Zion Still Sings

For Every Generation

Accompaniment Edition

Abingdon Press
Nashville, Tennessee

ZION STILL SINGS
Accompaniment Edition

Copyright © 2007 Abingdon Press

All rights reserved.

This book is printed on recycled, acid-free paper.

ISBN 978-0-687-33537-4

07 08 09 10 11 12 13 14 15 16 — 10 9 8 7 6 5 4 3 2 1

MANUFACTURED IN THE UNITED STATES OF AMERICA

Contents

Foreword

More than twenty-five years ago, in 1981, *Songs of Zion* was published and became a favorite of people and congregations in many denominations across the nation and around the world. Like previous collections of Christian music, it included treasured melodies and texts of deep and hallowed memory. The songs brought to mind days gone by and people who touched and shaped lives. It also contained expressions of the faith wrapped in fresh renderings sung by a new generation of Christians. The songs sprang largely from the Black religious experience, and the life and legacy of African Americans. Nevertheless, the message of pain, suffering, hope, and salvation resonated with people of many racial and ethnic backgrounds, who embraced the selections in *Songs of Zion* and found meaning and inspiration in them. In the end, songs belong uniquely to those who sing them.

Every generation sings its song of Zion, praising God in the sanctuary. And for twenty-five years, new songs have been pouring forth. Each new generation creates songs borne out of its experiences and circumstances, not merely those of former generations and eras. Exciting new genres of music have emerged with their own message of joy, pain, suffering, challenge, and hope. Hence the need for a compilation that captures the songs and rhythms of the future/present even while linking them to more traditional songs that have stood the test of time—a resource entitled *Zion Still Sings: For Every Generation.*

For nearly three years, a generationally diverse group representing talented and gifted church musicians, clergy, composers, and theological school faculty members from across the church has worked together to produce a new collection of the songs of faith that captures the best musical practice and tradition in African American churches today. *Zion Still Sings* will encompass music that is new and different, as well as the old and familiar. The committee also commissioned the composition of new texts and new tunes.

With *Zion Still Sings,* we believe we have created another valuable resource for the church and for all Christians who are compelled to sing the songs of Zion. This new book is not intended to replace *Songs of Zion* or any of the rich variety of worship resources already available to help people sing their faith with enthusiasm. Instead, it offers a resource that contains songs that will aid the spiritual formation of the Body of Christ, that old ship of Zion, as we are firmly established in the twenty-first century.

It is our hope that congregations will learn to love and value *Zion Still Sings.* Perhaps there are those who have been looking for new melodies and rhythms and will find them here, thus being able to sing the songs of faith as never before. There may even be those who have never before sung the songs of a faith rooted in Jesus Christ. Perhaps they will hear these songs and be touched and inspired by the music and message, so much so that they will choose to be numbered among the singing faithful.

In a world of continued strife, brokenness, despair, and hopelessness, we trust that this new songbook will be further evidence that even in such a world—for every generation—*Zion Still Sings!*

Bishop Woodie W. White, Retired
Chairperson

Preface

The work of this project began during the 2000–2004 quadrennial with the positing of such an idea to Neil Alexander, President and Publisher of The United Methodist Publishing House. Following the widespread acceptance across ecumenical lines and the continuing sales of *Songs of Zion* more than twenty years after its first printing, the project to contemporize and expand musical offerings in a new songbook was met with a great degree of interest and support.

The gathering of this collection of songs and music of *Zion Still Sings: For Every Generation* has been a labor of love and an act of worship for the Editorial Committee. During the last two years, the Committee members considered trends in African American worship, heard from numerous others through their participation in surveys, relied on our personal instincts and experiences, and benefited from the insights and wisdom of an ecumenical group of expert consultants, as we poured over hundreds of wonderful songs seeking to honor our purpose statement for this collection.

In the spirit of honoring and preserving the richness and inclusiveness of our African American musical heritage in worship:

1. *This resource will celebrate the diversity of styles, genres, and performance practices that are rendered in praise to God.*
2. *This resource will offer up new music that will inspire and challenge persons to see God with new eyes.*
3. *This resource will seek to motivate those outside the church to come to know God.*
4. *This resource will not compromise the theological and biblical integrity of the church.*
5. *This resource, in the spirit of Matthew 28:19, will serve as a motivating force for persons to "do" the gospel.*

I acknowledge with grateful appreciation the pioneering efforts of those who gave us *Songs of Zion* and the members of the Editorial Committee of *Zion Still Sings: For Every Generation* who are determined to keep Zion singing.

Bishop Woodie W. White, Chair	Dean B. McIntyre
*William B. McClain, Chair of Texts	Mark A. Miller
*Cynthia Wilson, Chair of Tunes	Marilyn E. Thornton, Music Editor
Gennifer Brooks	Charlene Ugwu, Project Manager
Cecilia L. Clemons	Bob MacKendree, Music Resources, UMPH
Marlon Hall	Bill Gnegy, Music Resources, UMPH
Monya Davis Logan	Gary Smith, Music Resources, UMPH
Henry Masters, Sr.	

Finally, we are grateful to all who have helped in any way.

Myron F. McCoy
General Editor

*Members of *Songs of Zion* Editorial Committee

Just a Few Words

God meets us in every situation, for every generation, and in every location. That's what we mean by *Zion Still Sings*. Zion is where we meet God. When heads were bowed down with the oppression of slavery, a song would come forth such as "Guide My Feet" or "I Want Jesus to Walk with Me" and God would be there, lifting heads and hearts. God was in the hush arbors, the segregated galleries, the mission churches, and in the churches built from used bricks, as the community sang hymns such as "At the Cross" and "Yield Not to Temptation," gaining the assurance that God's kingdom was inclusive.

God was present in Historically Black Colleges and Universities where many who contributed to this collection received training and teach: Howard University (Washington, DC), Bluefield State (WV), Dillard (LA), Bethune-Cookman College (FL), Interdenominational Theological Center (GA), and Tennessee State University. God was present when doors began to open, giving opportunities to learn and teach at places like Juilliard (NY), Peabody Conservatory (MD), Drew University (NJ), Eastman School of Music (NY), Vanderbilt Divinity School (TN), and many other fine state and private institutions.

Zion Still Sings because just as God was present during the Great Migration with Charles Tindley and Kenneth Morris, just as God was present during the Civil Rights Movement when we sang "Ain't Gonna Let Nobody Turn Me 'Round," God meets the current generation in the streets of our 21st-century world. God will meet you with "It's Incredible," using call and response in a way that the ancestors would never have dreamed. God will be present as you rap out "Heavenly Father" and interpret the prayer of Jesus for post-moderns. God will meet you in the contemporary jazz tones of a song for ushers, "Step," and the upbeat, 12-bar blues of "All Around Me!" a song that echoes the biblical truth that God is so high, so low, and so wide. God is inclusive.

There were many contributors to *Zion Still Sings* with submissions from every location, situation, and generation—truly a community effort. The songbook has two editions, Pew and Accompaniment. The Pew Edition has all vocals needed for congregational participation with specific instructions concerning songs that may be linked in medleys. The Accompaniment Edition includes piano accompaniment, synthesizer, and percussion parts. Some songs are exactly the same in both editions, usually four-part hymn style. Thanks and acknowledgments to the Music Resources Unit at Abingdon Press and to a community of gifted and competent musicians, who composed, transcribed, arranged, edited, and typeset music. The production team included:

William S. Moon	Julianne Eriksen
Allen Tuten	Gary Alan Smith
Charlene Ugwu (Project Manager)	Bob MacKendree
Bill Gnegy	Debi Tyree

May you enjoy the fruit of this labor of love, *Zion Still Sings: For Every Generation*.

Marilyn E. Thornton,
Music Editor for *Zion Still Sings*

All Around Me!

Where can I go from your spirit? Or where can I flee from your presence? If I ascend to heaven, you are there;
if I make my bed in Sheol, you are there. If I take the wings of the morning and settle at the farthest limits of the sea,
even there your hand shall lead me, and your right hand shall hold me fast. (Psalm 139:7-10)

Very upbeat (♩ = 160)

1. God is high, God is low, God is wide and he loves me so, all a-round me, oh yes, all a-round me. So high, so low, so wide, and he loves me so. ____
2. God is here, God is there, God is great and he's ev-ery-where all a-round me, oh yes, all a-round me. So here, so there, so great, ev-ery-where. _
3. God is in, God is out, God's so good that it makes me shout all a-round me, oh yes, all a-round me. So in, so out, so good that it makes me shout. _

Alternate bass line

See Performance Notes.
WORDS: Cecilia Olusola Tribble
MUSIC: Cecilia Olusola Tribble
© 2006 Cecilia Olusola Tribble

2

All My Days

In your book were written all the days that were formed for me, when none of them as yet existed. (Psalm 139:16)

1. You know my words, be - fore they're said. You
(2. If) I should fly be - yond the dawn, the
(3. Our) ev - ery thought, each word we say, the
(4. O) mend my heart and free my voice. From

know my need and I am fed. You give me life. You
dark - ness will not o - ver - come. If I lie down in
whole of time, the pres - ent day, are held with - in your
sin re - leased, I will re - joice. O search me, Lord, my

See Performance Notes.

WORDS: Laurie Zelman
MUSIC: Mark A. Miller

HIXON
88.88

3

Psalm 8: O Lord, How Excellent

O LORD, our Sovereign, how majestic is your name in all the earth! (Psalm 8:1a)

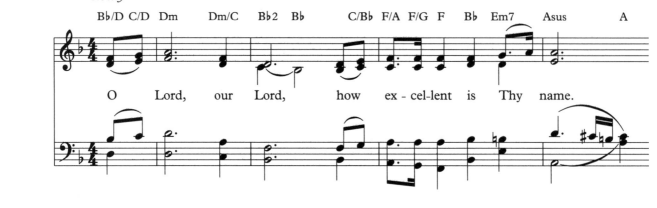

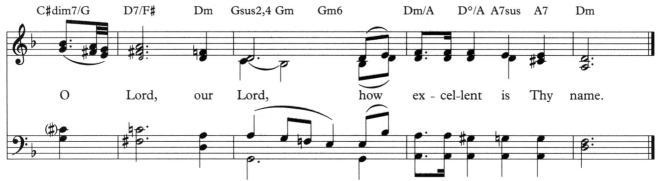

WORDS: Richard Smallwood (Ps. 8:1)
MUSIC: Richard Smallwood, arr. by Stephen Key

© 1984 Century Oak Publishing Group/Richwood Music, admin. by MCS America, Inc./Brentwood-Benson Music Publishing

4

Your Great Name We Praise
(Immortal, Invisible)

To the King of the ages, immortal, invisible, the only God, be honor and glory
forever and ever. Amen. (1 Timothy 1:17)

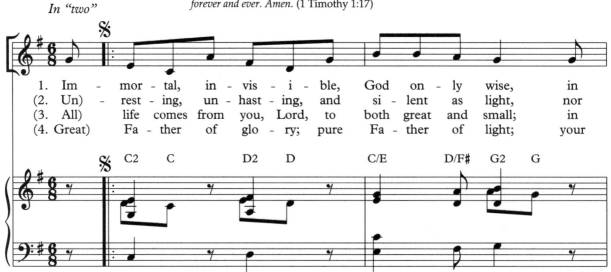

WORDS: Walter Chalmers Smith, adapt. by Bob Kauflin
MUSIC: Bob Kauflin

Music © 2001 Sovereign Grace Praise, admin. in the U.S. and Canada by Integrity's Praise! Music

I Lift Up My Hands

5

So I will bless you as long as I live; I will lift up my hands and call on your name. (Psalm 63:4)

Very slowly

Fa - ther, I love you. My heart is filled with de -

sire to see. Your pow - er and glo - ry cov-er the earth as the

wa - ters clothe the sea. I am sur - round - ed by the for - tress of God

WORDS: Israel Houghton and Ricardo Sanchez
MUSIC: Israel Houghton and Ricardo Sanchez, arr. by Linda Furtado and Zeke Listenbee

What a Mighty God We Serve

What god in heaven or on earth can perform deeds and mighty acts like yours! (Deuteronomy 3:24*b*)

WORDS: Donn Thomas
MUSIC: Donn Thomas
© 1983 Ron Harris Music

Hal - le-lu, hal-le-lu - jah! Hal-le-lu, hal-le-lu - jah!

Hal-le - lu, hal-le-lu - jah! What a might - y God we serve.

2. Let us sing

Awesome God

And he will reign forever and ever. (Revelation 11:15c)

Moderately fast (♩ = 120)

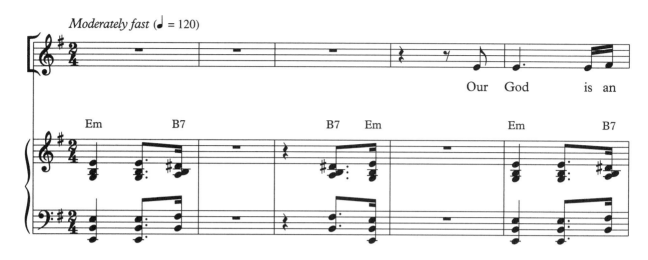

Our God is an

awe-some God, he reigns from heav-en a-bove with wis - dom,

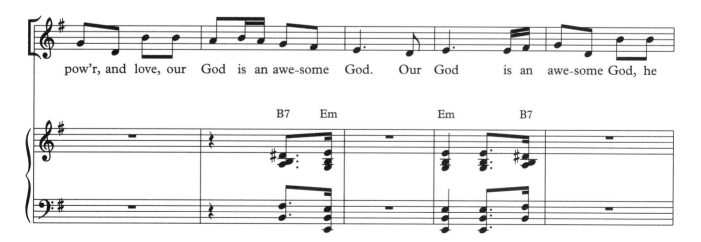

pow'r, and love, our God is an awe-some God. Our God is an awe-some God, he

WORDS: Richard Mullins
MUSIC: Richard Mullins, from Kirk Franklin, arr. by Cynthia Wilson

© 1988 BMG Songs, Inc.; arr. © 2000 GIA Publications, Inc.

AWESOME GOD
Irregular

Almighty

Great and amazing are your deeds, Lord God the Almighty!
Just and true are your ways. (Revelation 15:3b)

27

Bless the Lord

Bless the LORD, O my soul, and all that is within me, bless his holy name. (Psalm 103:1)

WORDS: Psalm 103:1
MUSIC: Andraé Crouch, arr. by Nolan Williams, Jr.

BLESS HIS HOLY NAME
Irregular

10

Clap Your Hands

Clap your hands, all you peoples; shout to God with loud songs of joy. (Psalm 47:1)

WORDS: Handt Hanson and Paul Murakami

MUSIC: Handt Hanson and Paul Murakami

CLAP YOUR HANDS

Irregular

song! _____ God is great! We

D.C. al Fine

praise our God with song! _____

Great Jehovah

11

Hallelujah! For the Lord our God the Almighty reigns. (Revelation 19:6b)

Reverently

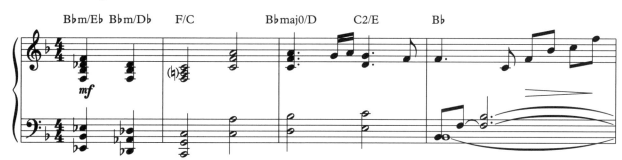

WORDS: Colette Coward
MUSIC: Colette Coward

12

Because of Who You Are

Let them give glory to the LORD, and declare his praise in the coastlands. (Isaiah 42:12)

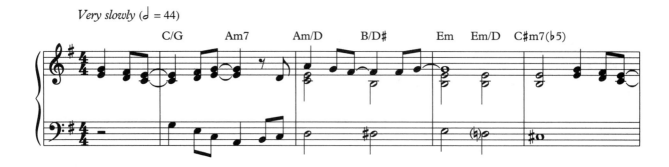

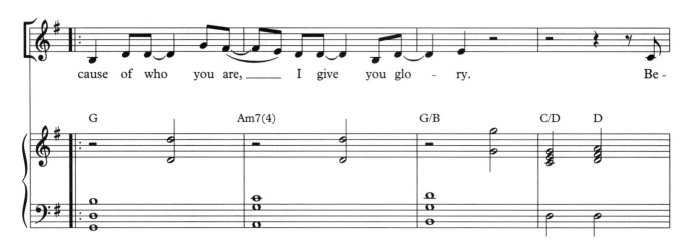

WORDS: Martha Munizzi
MUSIC: Martha Munizzi, arr. by William S. Moon

*Melody is in middle note.

Shout Medley
What a Mighty God We Serve

And all the angels … fell on their faces before the throne and worshiped God. (Revelation 7:11)

13

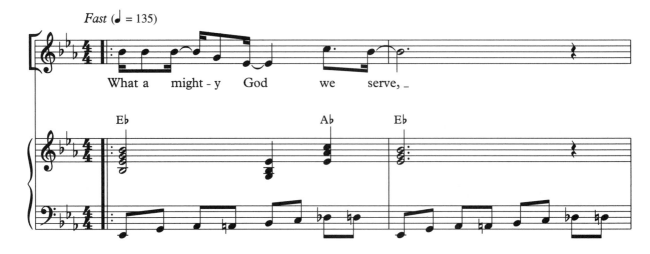

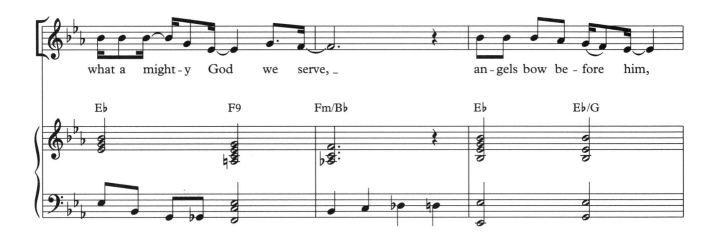

See Performance Notes.

WORDS: Trad. African folk song
MUSIC: Trad. African folk song, arr. by Stephen Key, this arr. by Oscar Dismuke

14

Shout

My lips will shout for joy when I sing praises to you. (Psalm 71:23a)

WORDS: Martha Munizzi
MUSIC: Martha Munizzi, arr. by Oscar Dismuke

shout un-to God for the vic-to-ry. Hey, hey,

give the Lord a shout of praise._ So I will

Shout to the Lord

15

Make a joyful noise to the LORD, all the earth;
break forth into joyous song and sing praises. (Psalm 98:4)

Shout to the Lord all the earth _ let us sing pow-er and maj - es-ty, praise _

See Performance Notes.

WORDS: Darlene Zschech
MUSIC: Darlene Zschech, arr. by Oscar Dismuke

ZSCHECH
Irregular

I Worship You, Almighty God /
There Is None Like You

I am God, and there is no one like me. (Isaiah 46:9b)

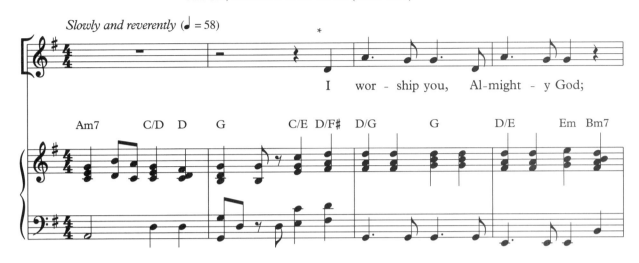

I wor - ship you, Al-might - y God;

there is none like you. I wor - ship you, O Prince of Peace;

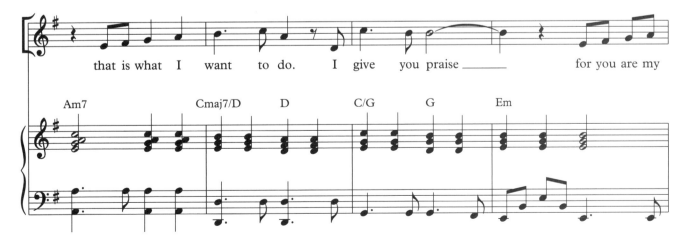

that is what I want to do. I give you praise _____ for you are my

*WORDS: Sondra Corbett
MUSIC: Sondra Corbett, arr. by Jonathan Cole Dow

righ - teous-ness. _____ I wor - ship you, Al-might - y God;

there is none like you. There is none like _

_ you, no one else can touch my heart like you do;

I could search for all e - ter-ni-ty long and find _ there is none like _____ you.

**WORDS: Lenny Leblanc
MUSIC: Lenny Leblanc

End of **Shout Medley**

God Made Me

God saw everything that God had made, and indeed, it was very good. (Genesis 1:31, alt.)

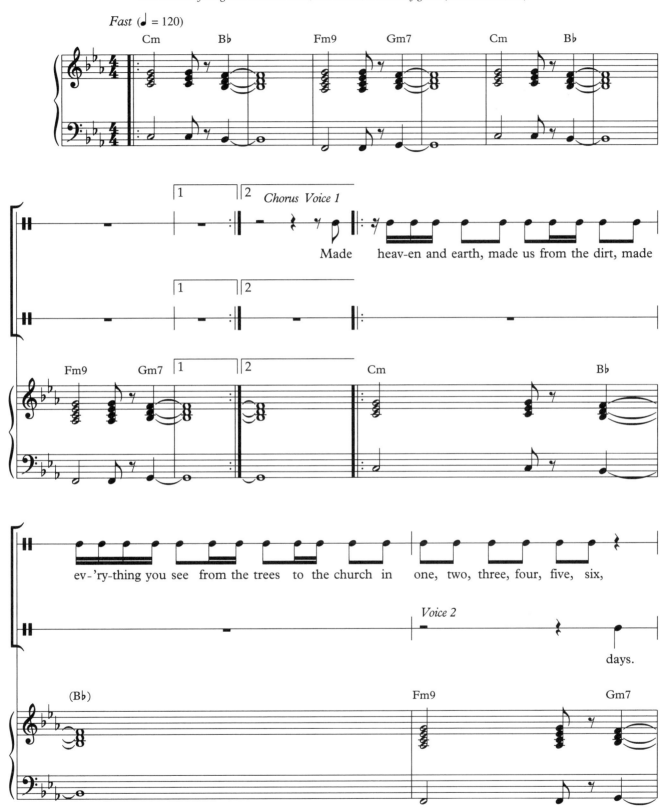

See Performance Notes.

WORDS: Frederick Burchell
MUSIC: Frederick Burchell and Kyle Lovett
© 2007 B4 Entertainment

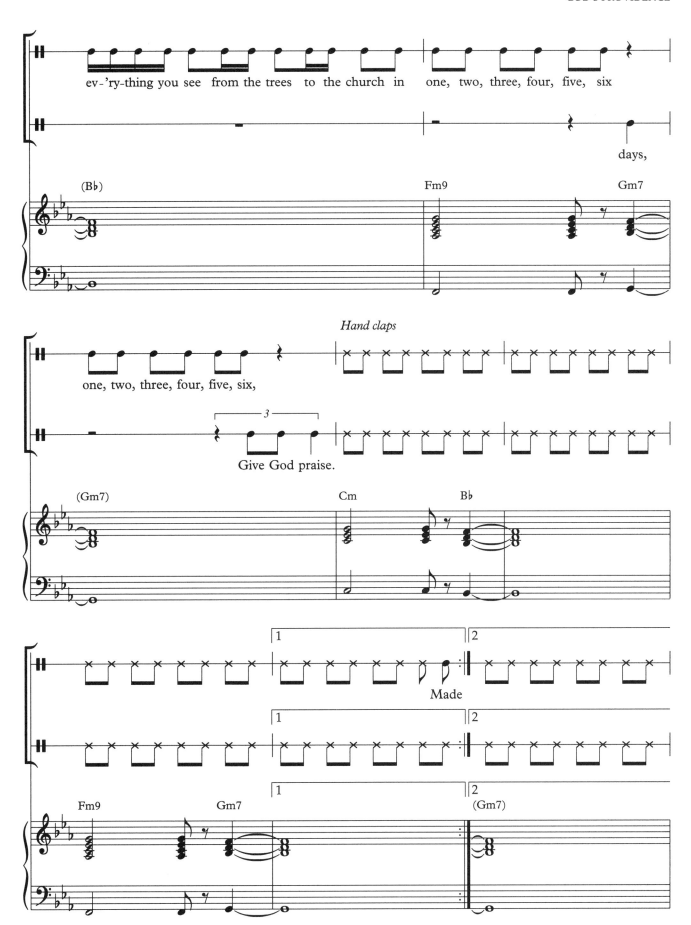

God Made Me

Drum Set

Fast (♩ = 120)

MUSIC: Frederick Burchell and Kyle Lovett

18

God Is Good, All the Time

O give thanks to the LORD, for he is good; for his steadfast love endures forever. (Psalm 107:1)

God is good, God is good all the time. God is

good, God is good all the time.

1. In   our doubts, hopes and fears,   joys and
2. When there's no   one   to   share   our de-
3. When there's love   to   be found   all   a-
4. When our sor - row we bring, let   us
5. As   our thanks   and   our praise   now we

tears,
spair,
round,   God   is   good,   God   is   good   all   the   time.
sing:
raise,

GOD IS GOOD
9.9.9.9.

I Will Bless Thee, O Lord

And now, our God, we give thanks to you and praise your glorious name. (1 Chronicles 29:13)

WORDS: Esther Watanabe
MUSIC: Esther Watanabe, arr. by Nolan Williams, Jr.

© 1970 New Song Music; arr. © 2000 GIA Publications, Inc.

I Will Celebrate Medley
I Will Celebrate

O sing to the LORD a new song; sing to the LORD, all the earth. (Psalm 96:1)

WORDS: Linda Duvall
MUSIC: Linda Duvall, arr. by Cynthia Wilson

21

I Will Sing of the Mercies
of the Lord Forever

Let your mercy come to me, that I may live. (Psalm 119:77a)

I will sing of the mer-cies of the Lord for - ev-er. I will sing. I will sing. I will sing of the mer-cies of the Lord for - ev - er. I will sing of the mer-cies of the Lord. With my mouth will I make known thy faith - ful-ness, thy faith - ful-ness. With my

*Omit if not performing medley.

WORDS: James H. Fillmore
MUSIC: James H. Fillmore, arr. by Cynthia Wilson

22

I Will Sing unto the Lord

"I will sing unto the LORD, for he has triumphed gloriously;
horse and the rider he has thrown into the sea." (Exodus 15:1*b*)

*May be sung as a canon.

See Performance Notes.

WORDS: Anon.
MUSIC: Anon., arr. by Cynthia Wilson

Arr. © 2007 Abingdon Press, admin. by The Copyright Co.

End of **I Will Celebrate Medley**

23

A Cause to Celebrate
A Medley of African Gospel Praise Songs
My grace is sufficient for you. (2 Corinthians 12:9a)

*That Priceless Grace

That price-less grace, that price-less grace that price-less grace which gave me life; Je-sus' life is price-less

*WORDS: Ghanaian praise song
MUSIC: Ghanaian praise song, transcribed and arr. by Newlove Annan

Arr. © 2007 Abingdon Press, admin. by The Copyright Co.

**WORDS: Ghanaian praise song
MUSIC: Ghanaian praise song, transcribed and arr. by Newlove Annan

Arr. © 2007 Abingdon Press, admin. by The Copyright Co.

**I Will Praise Him

Glorious

Sing forth the honour of his name; make his praise glorious. (Psalm 66:2 KJV)

When you come in-to his pres-ence lift-ing

up the name of Je - sus and you hear the mu - sic play - in' and you

WORDS: Martha Munizzi, Dan Munizzi, and Israel Houghton
MUSIC: Martha Munizzi, Dan Munizzi, and Israel Houghton, arr. by Oscar Dismuke

I was cre-at-ed to make your praise glo - ri-ous. _____

25   Glorious Is the Name of Jesus

Blessed be your glorious name, which is exalted above all blessing and praise. (Nehemiah 9:5b)

Glo - rious is the name of Je - sus, prais - es to his name. Oh,

glo - rious and righ - teous and ho - y is his name, Oh,

See Performance Notes.

WORDS: Dr. Robert J. Fryson
MUSIC: Dr. Robert J. Fryson
© 1982 Bob Jay Music Co.

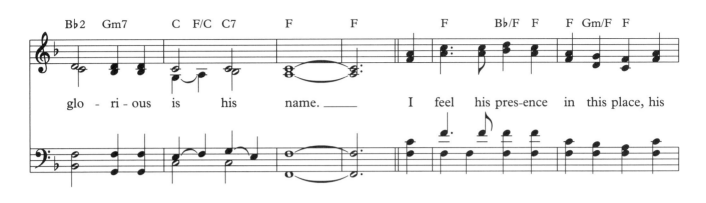

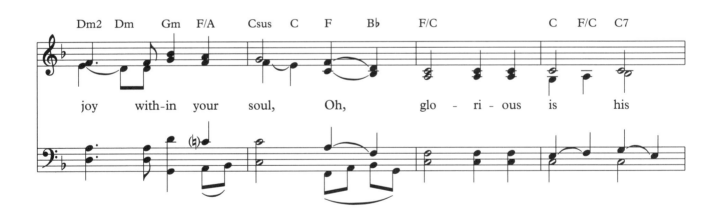

77

26 How Majestic Is Your Name

O LORD, our Sovereign, how majestic is your name in all the earth! (Psalm 8:9)

WORDS: Michael W. Smith
MUSIC: Michael W. Smith

HOW MAJESTIC
Irregular

27

Jesus, Name above All Names

Therefore God also highly exalted him
and gave him the name that is above every name. (Philippians 2:9)

NAME ABOVE ALL NAMES
Irregular

I Sing Praises to Your Name

I will be glad and exult in you; I will sing praise to your name. (Psalm 9:2)

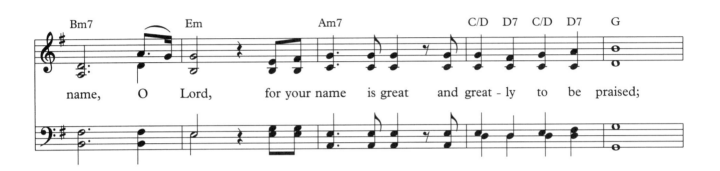

2. I give glory to your name …

WORDS: Terry MacAlmon
MUSIC: Terry MacAlmon

I SING PRAISES
Irregular

Name Medley
Praise the Name of Jesus

Lord, who will not fear and glorify your name? (Revelation 15:4)

29

See Performance Notes.

WORDS: Roy Hicks, Jr.
MUSIC: Roy Hicks, Jr.

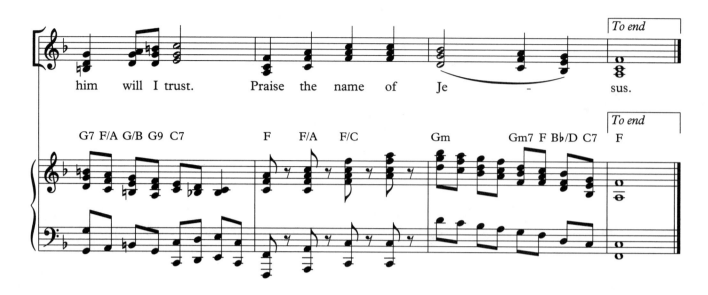

him will I trust. Praise the name of Je - sus.

30

Bless That Wonderful Name

Then everyone who calls on the name of the Lord shall be saved. (Acts 2:21)

sus.*

*Omit if not performing medley.

See Performance Notes.

WORDS: Congregational praise song
MUSIC: Congregational praise song, vocal arr. by Cynthia Wilson, piano arr. by William S. Moon

1. Bless that won-der-ful name of Je - sus!
2. Pow - er in the name of Je - sus!

Bless that won-der-ful name of Je - sus!
Pow - er in the name of Je - sus!

Bless that won-der-ful name of Je - sus! No oth-er name I
Pow - er in the name of Je - sus! No oth-er name I

know!

know!

know!

31 His Name Is Wonderful

And he is named Wonderful Counselor, Mighty God, Everlasting Father, Prince of Peace. (Isaiah 9:6b)

See Performance Notes.

WORDS: Audrey Mieir
MUSIC: Audrey Mieir, vocal arr. by Cynthia Wilson, piano arr. by William S. Moon

32

In the Name of Jesus

If in my name you ask me for anything, I will do it. (John 14:14)

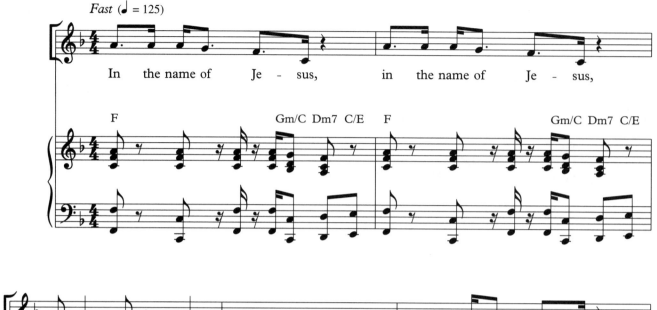

In the name of Je - sus, in the name of Je - sus,

We have the vic - to - ry! In the name of Je - sus,

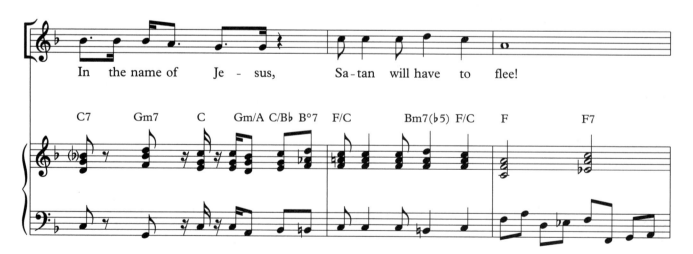

In the name of Je - sus, Sa - tan will have to flee!

See Performance Notes.

WORDS: Congregational praise song
MUSIC: Congregational praise song, vocal arr. by Cynthia Wilson, piano arr. by William S. Moon

Tell me, who can stand be - fore us,

when we call on that great name? Je - sus! Je - sus!

Pre - cious Je - sus! We have the vic - to - ry!

33 Jesus, What a Beautiful Name

She will bear a son, and you are to name him Jesus,
for he will save his people from their sins. (Matthew 1:21)

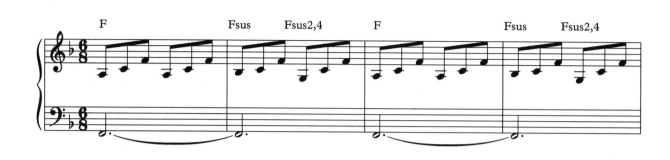

1. Je - sus, what a beau - ti - ful name, ____
2. Je - sus, what a beau - ti - ful name, ____
3. Je - sus, what a beau - ti - ful name, ____

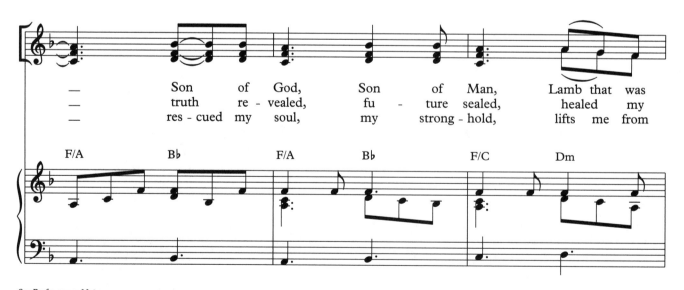

— Son of God, Son of Man, Lamb that was
— truth re - vealed, fu - ture sealed, healed my
— res - cued my soul, my strong - hold, lifts me from

See Performance Notes.

WORDS: Tanya Riches
MUSIC: Tanya Riches, arr. by Cynthia Wilson

End of **Name Medley**

34 In the Sanctuary

Lift up your hands to the holy place, and bless the Lord. (Psalm 134:2)

See Performance Notes.

WORDS: Kurt Carr
MUSIC: Kurt Carr, piano arr. by Darryl Glenn Nettles

35 Praise Him

The LORD lives! Blessed be my rock, and exalted be my God,
the rock of my salvation. (2 Samuel 22:47)

WORDS: Donnie Harper
MUSIC: Donnie Harper, arr. by Stephen Key

1, 2 To verses
3
Fine
Gm F/C F/A Gm F♯dim7 Gm F/C Gm/C F/C C7 F F
Je - sus, bless-ed Sav - ior he's wor - thy to be praised. praised.
Verse
F Gm/F F C/G F/A Gm F/A Gm/B♭ F/C C7 F
1. From the ris - ing of the sun un - til the go - ing down of the same, he's
F Gm F/G Gm F/A Dm7 G G9 C
D.C.
wor - thy, Je - sus is wor - thy, he's wor - thy to be praised.
F C/G F/A Gm F/A Gm/B♭ F/C C7 F
2. God is our rock, hope of sal - va - tion; A
F Gm F/G Gm F/A Dm7 G G9 C
D.C.
strong de - liv-er-er in him will I al-ways trust.

36

The Glory Song
(I'm Gonna Lift You Up)

I glorified you on earth by finishing the work that you gave me to do. (John 17:4)

WORDS: Byron Cage
MUSIC: Byron Cage, arr. by Cynthia Wilson

I'm gon - na lift you up. I'm gon - na lift you up.

High Praise

37

My soul magnifies the Lord, and my spirit rejoices in God my Savior. (Luke 1:47)

Pre - cious, ho - ly bless - ed Sav - ior, you are wor - thy

to be praised. Heav - en and earth bow be - fore you, you are wor - thy

To repeat | *To end* | *To Special Chorus (next page)*

to be praised. to be praised. to be praised.

WORDS: Margaret Pleasant Douroux
MUSIC: Margaret Pleasant Douroux, arr. by Nolan Williams, Jr.

Special Chorus*

*Begin with soprano line, then add each part one at a time

Celebrator

But I will hope continually, and will praise you yet more and more. (Psalm 71:14)

I'm a cel-e-bra-tor of my cre-a-tor.

Look what God has done. Sent his on-ly Son

so that I could live, and I'm gon-na give

See Performance Notes.

WORDS: Toby Hill
MUSIC: Toby Hill, transcribed by Stephanie York Blue
© 2002 Toby Hill

Love You, Lord, Medley

I Love You, Lord, Today

For you were bought with a price; therefore glorify God in your body. (1 Corinthians 6:20)

39

WORDS: William F. Hubbard
MUSIC: William F. Hubbard

I Love You, Lord   40

I love you, O LORD, my strength. (Psalm 18:1)

WORDS: Laurie Klein
MUSIC: Laurie Klein, arr. by Nolan Williams, Jr.

I Really Love the Lord

We love because he first loved us. (1 John 4:19)

WORDS: Jimmy Dowell
MUSIC: Jimmy Dowell, arr. by Nolan Williams, Jr.

End of **Love You, Lord, Medley**

Lord, Reign in Me

42

And let the peace of Christ rule in your hearts. (Colossians 3:15a)

See Performance Notes.

WORDS: Brenton Brown
MUSIC: Brenton Brown, arr. by William S. Moon

43 You Inhabit the Praises of Your People

But thou art holy, O thou that inhabitest the praises of Israel. (Psalm 22:3 KJV)

WORDS: Regina Hoosier
MUSIC: Regina Hoosier

Greater

For the one who is in you is greater than the one who is in the world. (1 John 4:4*b*)

WORDS: Twila McBride-LaBar
MUSIC: Twila McBride-LaBar

117

And the Word Is God

45

In the beginning was the Word, and the Word was with God, and the Word was God. (John 1:1)

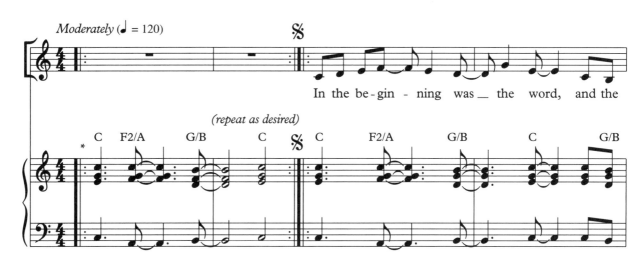

In the be-gin - ning was the word, and the

word was God. Ev-ery-day life is spo - ken and the

word is God. God's plan of sav-ing grace for you and me is

*Right hand may be played one octave lower than written.

WORDS: Cecilia Olusola Tribble
MUSIC: Cecilia Olusola Tribble

© 2007 Cecilia Olusola Tribble

46

The Only One

Your word is a lamp to my feet and a light to my path. (Psalm 119:105)

You mean more to me than an-y words could say. _ You il-lu-mi-nate my

path and lead the way. _ Like a star you shine so bright that I can see _

WORDS: Antonio Phelon
MUSIC: Antonio Phelon, arr. by William S. Moon

47

Breathe

When he said this, he breathed on them and said to them, "Receive the Holy Spirit." (John 20:22)

This is the air __ I breathe, this is the air __ I breathe,

your ho - ly pres - ence, liv - ing in me, __

this is my dai - ly bread, this is my dai - ly bread,

WORDS: Marie Barnett
MUSIC: Marie Barnett, arr. by Mark A. Miller

BREATHE
Irregular

48 Santo, Santo, Santo

Glory in his holy name; let the hearts of those who seek the LORD rejoice. (1 Chronicles 16:10)

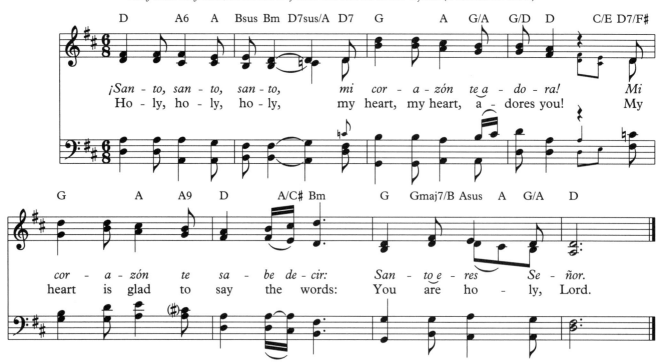

WORDS: Argentine folk song
MUSIC: Argentine folk song, arr. by Nolan Williams, Jr.

Let It Rise

Arise, shine; for your light has come, and the glory of the LORD has risen upon you. (Isaiah 60:1)

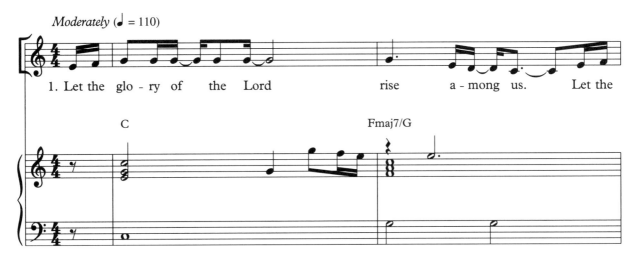

WORDS: Holland Davis
MUSIC: Holland Davis, arr. by Linda Furtado

Show Teeth

Be glad in the LORD and rejoice, O righteous, and shout for joy,
all you upright in heart. (Psalm 32:11)

See Performance Notes.

WORDS: Toby Hill
MUSIC: Luke Austin, transcribed by Stephanie York Blue
© 2005 Toby Hill

51

Wailing into Dancing

You have turned my mourning into dancing;
you have taken off my sackcloth and clothed me with joy. (Psalm 30:11)

You turned my wail-ing in-to danc-ing, took a-

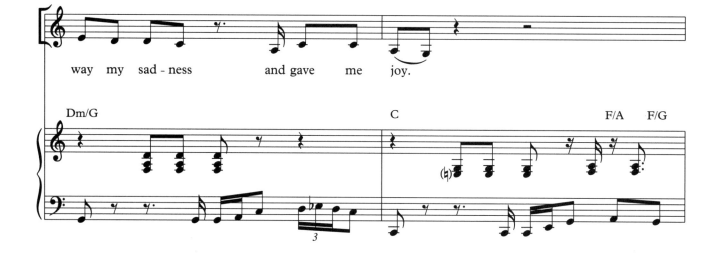

way my sad-ness and gave me joy.

You made my heart sing, I can't keep si-lent. I will

WORDS: Donn Thomas
MUSIC: Donn Thomas, transcribed by William S. Moon

Incredible

For to me, living is Christ and dying is gain. (Philippians 1:21)

See Performance Notes.

WORDS: Brian C. Wilson
MUSIC: Leon Lewis and Brian C. Wilson, transcribed by Stephanie York Blue

153

reach   and you   grab hold.   It's   a - reach   and you   grab hold.   We

reach,   we reach,   we reach and you grab hold.   We

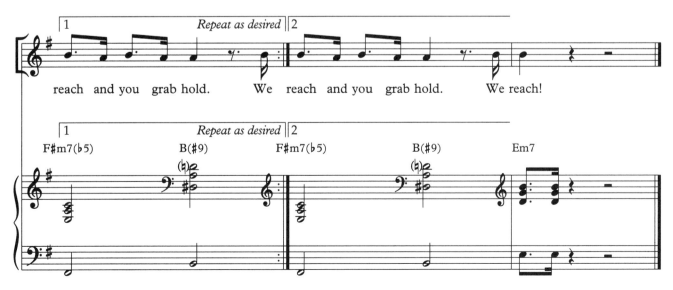

reach   and you   grab hold.   We   reach   and you   grab hold.   We reach!

53

All Hail King Jesus

"It is I, Jesus … I am the root and the descendant of David, the bright morning star." (Revelation 22:16)

All hail King Je - sus! All hail Em-man - u - el,

— King of kings, Lord of lords, bright Morn-ing Star.

African American churches often use this slower tempo.

See Performance Notes.

WORDS: Dave Moody
MUSIC: Dave Moody

KING JESUS
Irregular

He Came Down

He came to what was his own … but to all who received him …
he gave power to become children of God. (John 1:11-12)

He came down that we may have *love; he came down that we may have love; he
came down that we may have love, hal-le-lu-jah for-ev-er-more.
Why did he come?

*Substitute peace, joy, hope, life, etc.

WORDS: Cameroon traditional
MUSIC: Cameroon traditional; trans. and arr. by John L. Bell

55 Already Here

The LORD is in his holy temple. (Psalm 11:4a)

Slowly

Group 1
(or solo)

We watch and we wait, — Lord, we an-ti-ci-pate the

Group 2
(on repeat only)

ia.

ad lib freely

WORDS: Brian C. Wilson
MUSIC: Brian C. Wilson, transcribed by Stephanie York Blue

Amen Siakudumisa

All the people answered, "Amen, Amen."
Then they bowed their heads and worshiped the LORD. (Nehemiah 8:6)

WORDS: Trad. Xhosa (South Africa); attr. to S. C. Molefe as taught by George Mxadana

MUSIC: Trad. Xhosa melody, as taught by George Mxadana, arr. by John L. Bell

MASITHI
Irregular

Arr. © 1990 The Iona Community (Scotland), GIA Publications, Inc., agent

(Omit last time.)

Ma - si - thi. ___
O sing now. __

A - men ba - wo, A - men si - a - ku - du - mi - sa.
A - men sing praise, A - men sing prais - es to the Lord.

wo, ba - wo, ba - wo si - a - ku - du - mi - sa.
name, O praise God's name, sing prais - es to the Lord.

Emmanuel

And they shall name him Emmanuel, which means, "God is with us." (Matthew 1:23*b*)

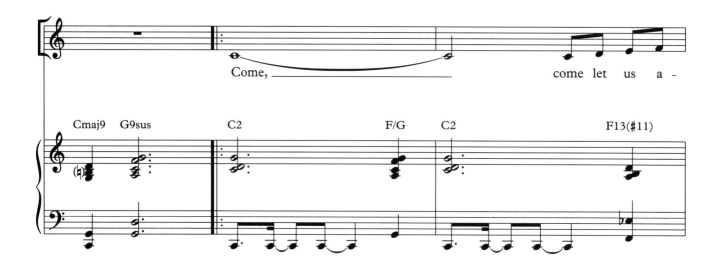

Come,_____ come let us a-

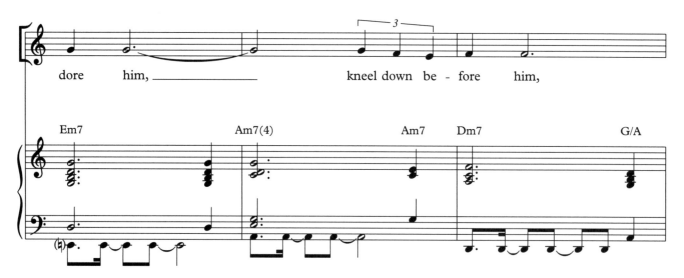

dore him,_____ kneel down be-fore him,

WORDS: Norman Hutchins and Jason White
MUSIC: Norman Hutchins and Jason White, arr. by Mark A. Miller

worship and a-dore him.

Come, come let us a-dore him, kneel down be-

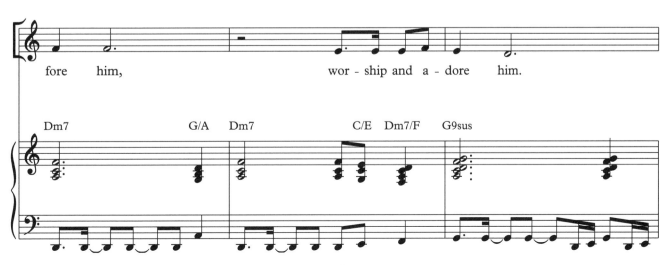

fore him, worship and a-dore him.

Bethlehem

In the time of King Herod … Jesus was born in Bethlehem of Judea. (Matthew 2:1a)

Beth - le -hem, __ Beth - le -hem, __ cit - y where __

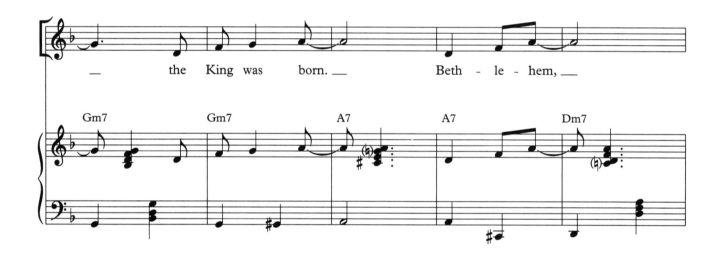

__ the King was born. __ Beth - le -hem, __

Beth - le -hem, __ Ma - ry had - a Je - sus on Christ -mas morn. __

WORDS: Marilyn E. Thornton
MUSIC: Marilyn E. Thornton
© 1985 Marilyn E. Thornton

59 Go, Tell It on the Mountain

When they saw this, they made known what had been told them about this child. (Luke 2:17)

Go, tell it on the moun - tain, o-ver the hills and ev - ery - where.

Go, tell it on the moun - tain that Je - sus Christ is born.

Fine

WORDS: African American spiritual, adapt. by John W. Work
MUSIC: African American spiritual, arr. by William S. Moon

GO TELL IT ON THE MOUNTAIN
Irregular with Refrain

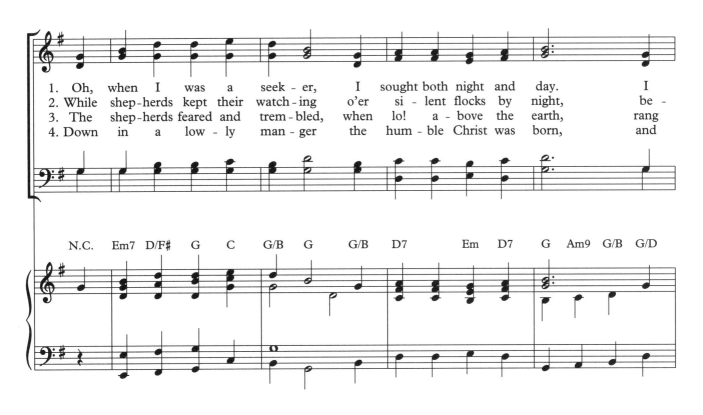

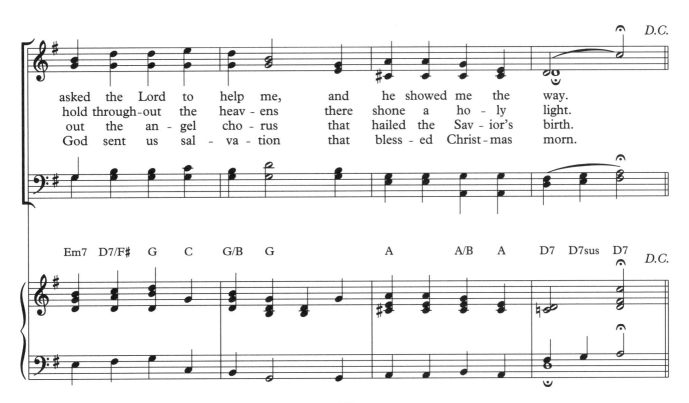

60
The Virgin Mary Had a Baby Boy

The virgin's name was Mary. (Luke 1:27b)

1. The
(2. The)
(3. The)
(4. The)

virgin Mary had a baby boy, the virgin Mary had a
angels sang when the baby was born, the angels sang when the
shepherds came where the baby was born, the shepherds came where the
Wise Men came where the baby was born, the Wise Men came where the

baby boy, the virgin Mary had a baby boy,
baby was born, the angels sang when the baby was born, and they
baby was born, the shepherds came where the baby was born,
baby was born, the Wise Men came where the baby was born,

Add percussion as desired.

WORDS: West Indian carol
MUSIC: West Indian carol, arr. by John Barnard

Arr. © 1945 Boosey & Co., Ltd., admin. by Boosey & Hawkes, Inc.

THE VIRGIN MARY
10 10.10 9 with Refrain

2. The
3. The
4. The

61 Heaven's Christmas Tree

Then the angel showed me the river of the water of life … .
On either side of the river, is the tree of life. (Revelation 22:1-2a)

1. I have heard of a tree, a great Christ - mas tree, it was
2. There is one I be - hold in let - ters of gold, It
3. There is one just a - bove, it's ti - tle is love, it is
4. An - oth - er I see, it must be for me, the
5. There are man - y I'm sure, but just this one more I

WORDS: Charles A. Tindley
MUSIC: Charles A. Tindley, arr. by Charles A. Tindley, Jr.

62

Jesus, the Light of the World

Again Jesus spoke to them, saying, "I am the light of the world." (John 8:12a)

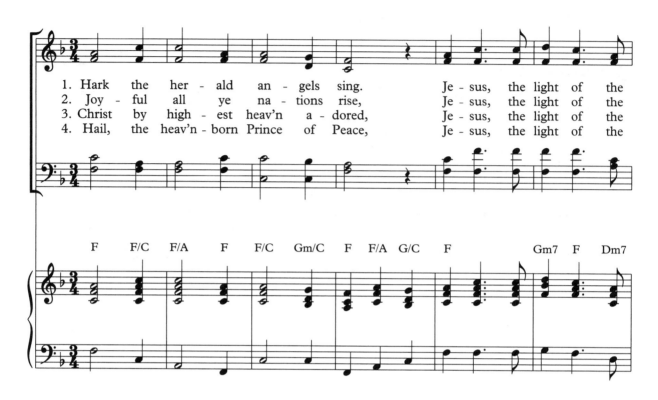

1. Hark the her - ald an - gels sing. Je - sus, the light of the
2. Joy - ful all ye na - tions rise, Je - sus, the light of the
3. Christ by high - est heav'n a - dored, Je - sus, the light of the
4. Hail, the heav'n - born Prince of Peace, Je - sus, the light of the

F F/C F/A F F/C Gm/C F F/A G/C F Gm7 F Dm7

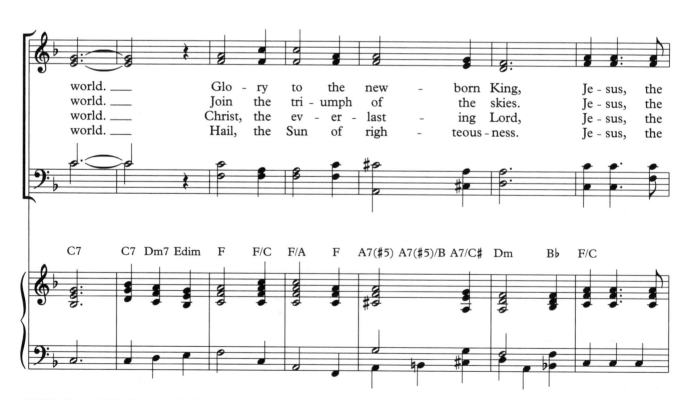

world. ___ Glo - ry to the new - born King, Je - sus, the
world. ___ Join the tri - umph of the skies. Je - sus, the
world. ___ Christ, the ev - er - last - ing Lord, Je - sus, the
world. ___ Hail, the Sun of righ - teous - ness. Je - sus, the

C7 C7 Dm7 Edim F F/C F/A F A7(♯5) A7(♯5)/B A7/C♯ Dm B♭ F/C

WORDS: George D. Elderkin, stanzas by Charles Wesley
MUSIC: George D. Elderkin, arr. by Evelyn Simpson-Curenton

WE'LL WALK IN THE LIGHT
7 7 7 7 with Refrain

Star-Child

For we observed his star at its rising, and have come to pay him homage. (Matthew 2:2b)

1. Star - Child earth - Child go - be - tween of God,
2. Street child, beat child, no place left to go,
3. Grown child, old child, mem - ory full of years,
4. Spared child, spoiled child, hav - ing, want - ing more,
5. Hope - for - peace Child, God's stu - pen - dous sign,

love Child, Christ Child, heav - en's light - ning rod,
hurt child, used child, no one wants to know,
sad child, lost child, sto - ry told in tears,
wise child, faith child, know - ing joy in store,
down - to - earth Child, Star of stars that shine,

This year, this year, let the day ar - rive when

Christ - mas comes for ev - ery - one, ev - ery - one a - live!

WORDS: Shirley Erena Murray
MUSIC: Carlton R. Young
© 1994 Hope Publishing Co.

STAR CHILD
45.45 with Refrain

Epiphany

And they knelt down and paid him homage.
Then, opening their treasure chests, they offered him gifts. (Matthew 2:11)

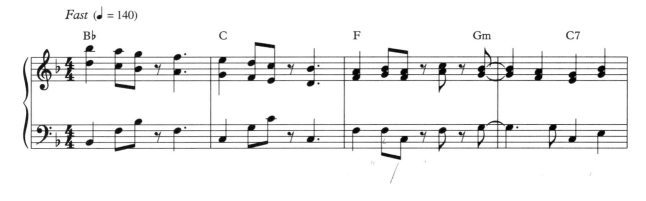

1. Wis - dom from a - far, ___ guid - ed by a star; ___
2. Light of our dark night, _ give us ho - ly sight.
3. Called to do your will, ___ Lord, we seek you still. ___

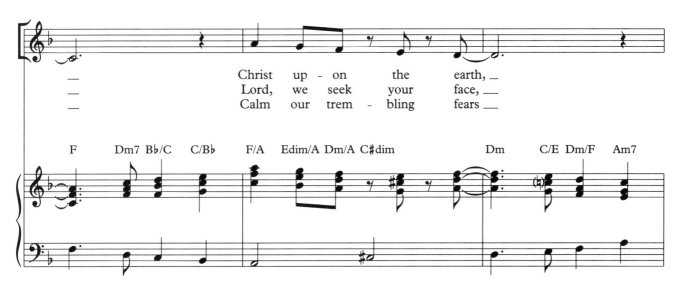

_ Christ up - on the earth, _
_ Lord, we seek your face, _
_ Calm our trem - bling fears _

Add percussion as desired.

WORDS: Gennifer Benjamin Brooks
MUSIC: William S. Moon

Words © 2007 Gennifer Benjamin Brooks; music © 2007 William S. Moon

He Is the Son of God

Truly, this man was God's Son. (Matthew 27:54b)

WORDS: Marilyn E. Thornton
MUSIC: Marilyn E. Thornton
© 1995 Marilyn E. Thornton

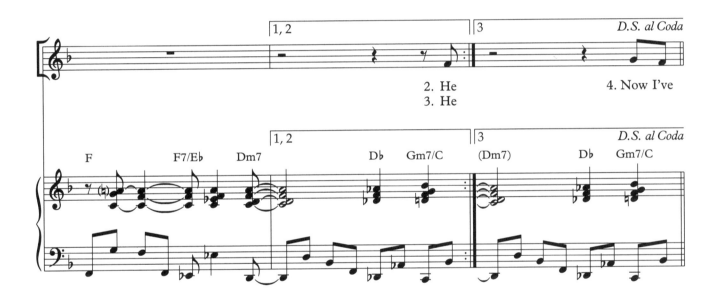

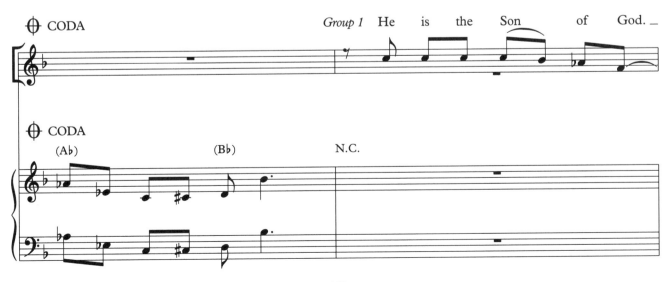

(Repeat this section as desired.)

He is the Son of God. —

Group 2

He is the Son of God. —

(Repeat this section as desired.)

F F7/E♭ Dm7 D♭ Gm7/C (A♭) (B♭)

66 Yield Not to Temptation

Blessed is anyone who endures temptation. (James 1:12a)

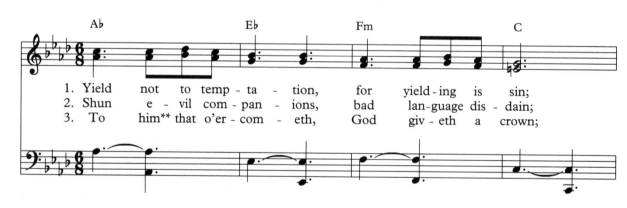

A♭ E♭ Fm C

1. Yield not to temp - ta - tion, for yield-ing is sin;
2. Shun e - vil com - pan - ions, bad lan-guage dis - dain;
3. To him** that o'er - com - eth, God giv - eth a crown;

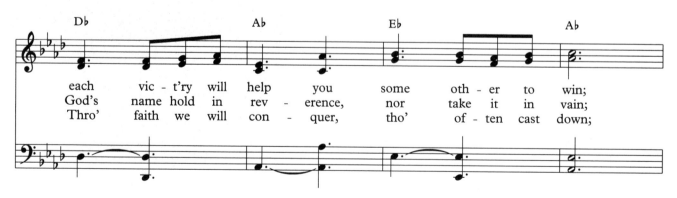

D♭ A♭ E♭ A♭

each vic - t'ry will help you some oth - er to win;
God's name hold in rev - erence, nor take it in vain;
Thro' faith we will con - quer, tho' of - ten cast down;

*"valiantly" may be substituted for "manfully"
**"those" may be substituted for "him"

WORDS: Horatio Richmond Palmer
MUSIC: Horatio Richmond Palmer

YIELD NOT
65 65 66 66 with Refrain

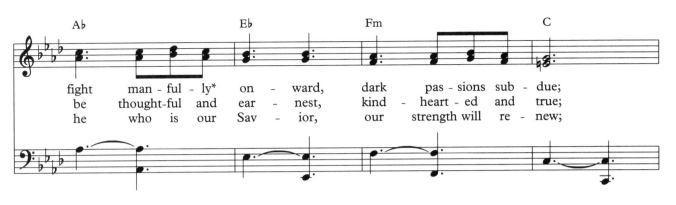

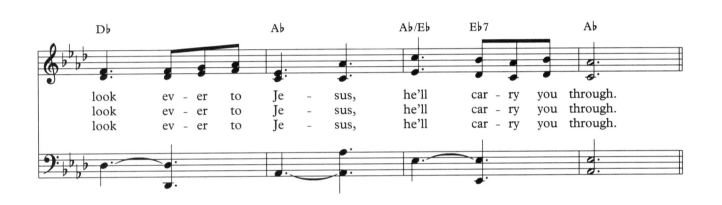

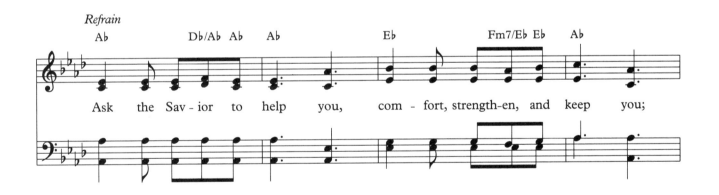

67

At the Cross

But God proves his love for us
in that while we still were sinners Christ died for us. (Romans 5:8)

WORDS: Isaac Watts and Ralph E. Hudson
MUSIC: Ralph E. Hudson, arr. by Oscar Dismuke
Arr. © 2007 Abingdon Press, admin. by The Copyright Co.

HUDSON
CM with Refrain

first saw the light, and the bur-den of my heart rolled a-way; it was
there by faith I re-ceived my sight, and now I am hap-py all the day.

God Weeps

68

For these things I weep; my eyes flow with tears …
my children are desolate, for the enemy has prevailed. (Lamentations 1:16)

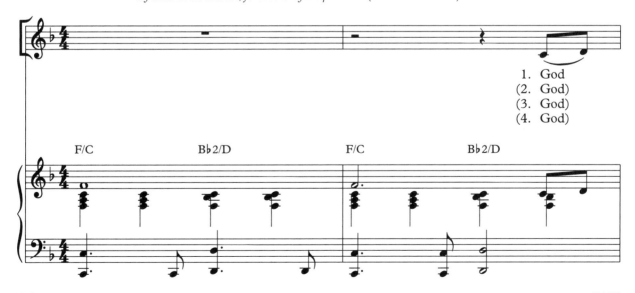

1. God
(2. God)
(3. God)
(4. God)

WORDS: Shirley Erena Murray
MUSIC: Mark A. Miller

DAKE
64.8 10

I Want Jesus to Walk with Me

69

"I will live in them and walk among them, and I will be their God, and they shall be my people." (2 Corinthians 6:16b)

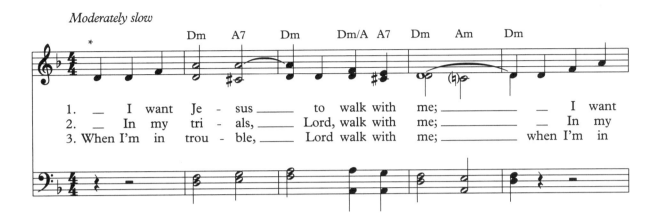

1. _ I want Je - sus _____ to walk with me; _____ _ I want
2. _ In my tri - als, _____ Lord, walk with me; _____ _ In my
3. When I'm in trou - ble, _____ Lord walk with me; _____ when I'm in

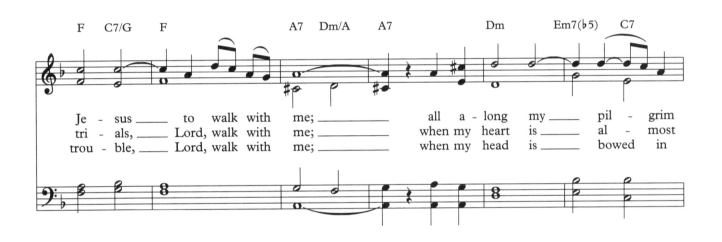

Je - sus _____ to walk with me; _____ all a - long my _____ pil - grim
tri - als, _____ Lord, walk with me; _____ when my heart is _____ al - most
trou - ble, _____ Lord, walk with me; _____ when my head is _____ bowed in

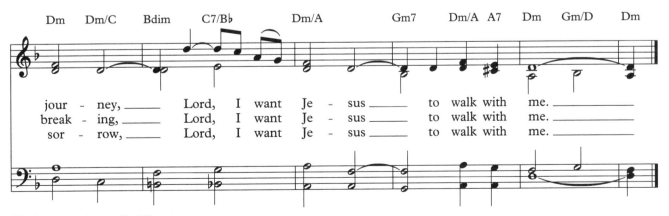

jour - ney, _____ Lord, I want Je - sus _____ to walk with me. _____
break - ing, _____ Lord, I want Je - sus _____ to walk with me. _____
sor - row, _____ Lord, I want Je - sus _____ to walk with me. _____

May be sung in unison or with ad lib parts.

WORDS: Trad. African American
MUSIC: Trad. African American

SOJOURNER
88 8 9

70

O Lord, Fix Me

Lord, if you choose, you can make me clean. (Matthew 8:2b)

O Lord, fix me, fix me, O Lord, fix me _____ make me thine in-stru-ment of love to-day.

WORDS: Eli Wilson, Jr.
MUSIC: Eli Wilson, Jr.

© Eli Wilson, Jr.

71

Nothing Between

For I am convinced that neither death, nor … anything else in all creation,
will be able to separate us from the love of God in Christ Jesus our Lord. (Romans 8:38-39)

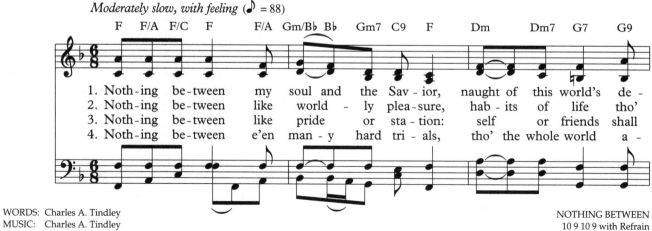

1. Noth-ing be-tween my soul and the Sav-ior, naught of this world's de-
2. Noth-ing be-tween like world-ly plea-sure, hab-its of life tho'
3. Noth-ing be-tween like pride or sta-tion: self or friends shall
4. Noth-ing be-tween e'en man-y hard tri-als, tho' the whole world a-

WORDS: Charles A. Tindley
MUSIC: Charles A. Tindley

Arr. © 1979 J. Edward Hoy

NOTHING BETWEEN
10 9 10 9 with Refrain

72

He Will Remember Me

Then he said, "Jesus, remember me when you come into your kingdom." (Luke 23:42)

1. When on the cross of Cal-vary the Lord was cru-ci-fied;
2. O, what a shame to kill him there on that rug-ged cross;
3. At his dear feet I'm kneel-ing, my sins I now con-fess;

the mob stood 'round a-bout him and mocked un-til he died.
but such a death was need-ed to res-cue all the lost.
I bow in deep re-pen-tance, my soul he'll sure-ly bless.

Two thieves were nailed be-side him to share the ag-o-ny,
His blood was made a ran-som to set the cap-tives free,
My blind-ed eyes he o-pens so that the light I see,

but one of them cried out to him, "O Lord re-mem-ber me."
I know that I'm in-clud-ed, and he will re-mem-ber me.
and when I reach the pearl-y gates, he will re-mem-ber me.

WORDS: Eugene M. Bartlett
MUSIC: Eugene M. Bartlett, arr. by Nolan Williams, Jr.

Arr. © 1976, renewed 2004 Albert E. Brumley & Sons, admin. by ICG

REMEMBER ME
76.76.76.86 with Refrain

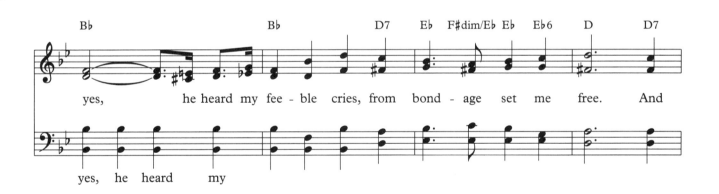

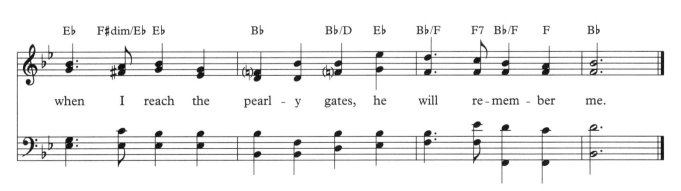

73

Calvary

And when they were come to the place, which is called Calvary,
there they crucified him. (Luke 23:33a KJV)

Very slowly (♩ = 40)

Cal - va - ry, _____ Cal - va - ry, Cal - va -

ry, _____ Cal - va - ry, Cal - va - ry, _____ Cal - va -

Fine

ry, _____ sure - ly he died on _____ Cal - va - ry. _____

N.C.

1. Ev - ery time I _____ think a-bout Je - sus, ev - ery
2. Don't you hear the _____ ham - mer ring - ing? Don't you
3. Don't you hear him _____ call - ing his Fa - ther? Don't you
4. Don't you hear him _____ say, "It is fin - ished"? Don't you
5. Je - sus fur - nished _____ my sal - va - tion. Je - sus
6. Sin - ner, do you _____ love my Je - sus? Sin - ner,

WORDS: African American spiritual
MUSIC: African American spiritual

CALVARY
LM with Refrain

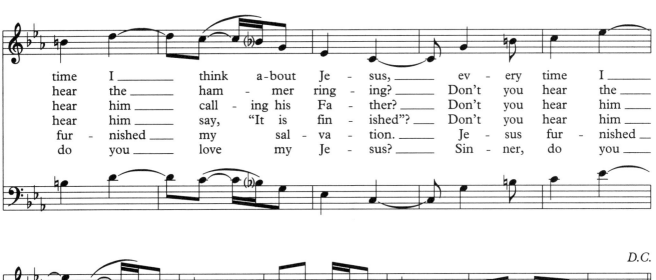

time I   think a-bout Je - sus,   ev - ery time I
hear the   ham - mer ring - ing?   Don't you hear the
hear him   call - ing his Fa - ther?   Don't you hear him
hear him   say, "It is fin - ished"?   Don't you hear him
fur - nished   my sal - va - tion.   Je - sus fur - nished
do you   love my Je - sus?   Sin - ner, do you

D.C.

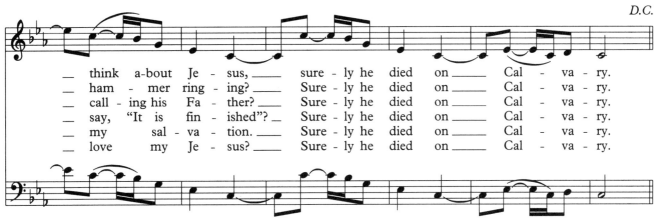

  think a-bout Je - sus,   sure - ly he died on   Cal - va - ry.
  ham - mer ring - ing?   Sure - ly he died on   Cal - va - ry.
  call - ing his Fa - ther?   Sure - ly he died on   Cal - va - ry.
  say, "It is fin - ished"?   Sure - ly he died on   Cal - va - ry.
  my sal - va - tion.   Sure - ly he died on   Cal - va - ry.
  love my Je - sus?   Sure - ly he died on   Cal - va - ry.

Lamb of God

"Here is the Lamb of God who takes away the sin of the world!" (John 1:29)

1. Your on-ly Son, no sin to hide, but you have sent him from your
(2. Your gift of) love they cru-ci-fied, they laughed and scorned him as he
(3. I was so) lost I should have died but you have brought me to your

side to walk up-on this guilt-y sod, and to be-
died: The hum-ble King they named a fraud, and sac-ri-
side to be led by your staff and rod, and to be

come the Lamb of God. 2. Your gift of God. O Lamb of
ficed the Lamb of
called a lamb of

WORDS: Twila Paris
MUSIC: Twila Paris
© 1985 Straightway Music/Mountain Spring Music (ASCAP), admin. by EMI CMG Publishing

LAMB OF GOD
LM with Refrain

God, sweet Lamb of God, I love the ho - ly Lamb of

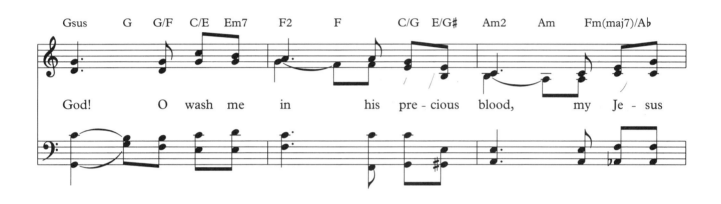

God! O wash me in his pre - cious blood, my Je - sus

Repeat ending   *Song ending*

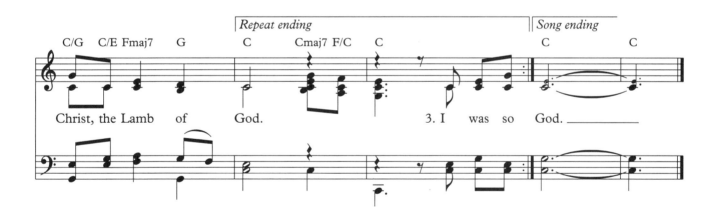

Christ, the Lamb of God.   3. I was so God. _____

The Lamb

"To the one seated on the throne and to the Lamb
be blessing and honor and glory and might forever and ever!" (Revelation 5:13b)

WORDS: Michael McKay
MUSIC: Michael McKay, arr. by William S. Moon
© Schaff Music Publishing

Halle, Halle, Halleluja

"I am the resurrection and the life.
Those who believe in me, even though they die, will live." (John 11:25)

Hal - le, hal - le, hal - le - lu - ja.
1. I AM the Rock of A - ges cleft for me;
2. I AM the Noth - ing in ___ my hands I bring;
3. I AM the Bread of Life, ___ feed on me;
4. I AM the Res - ur - rec - tion, live in me;

Claves

Maracas

Congas (Bongos)
Option 1

Congas (Bongos)
Option 2

WORDS: George Mulrain, Trinidad and Tobago
MUSIC: Caribbean folk song; arr. by Carlton R. Young

HALLE, HALLE
Irregular

77 Raised, He's Been Raised from the Dead

"Why do you look for the living among the dead? He is not here, but has risen." (Luke 24:5b)

See Performance Notes.

WORDS: Gennifer Benjamin Brooks
MUSIC: Monya Davis Logan

78

Friend

"When the Advocate comes, whom I will send to you from the Father,
the SPIRIT of truth … he will testify on my behalf." (John 15:26)

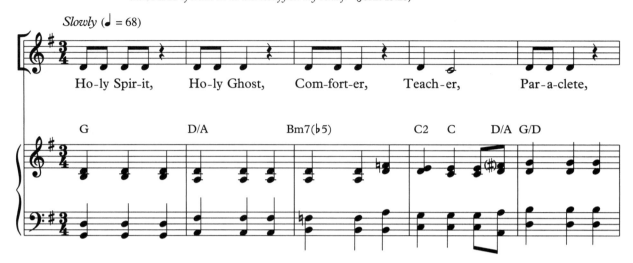

Ho-ly Spir-it, Ho-ly Ghost, Com-fort-er, Teach-er, Par-a-clete,

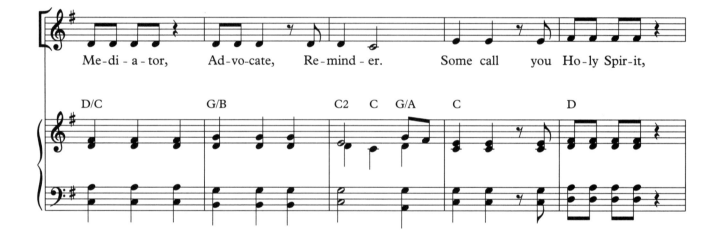

Me-di-a-tor, Ad-vo-cate, Re-mind-er. Some call you Ho-ly Spir-it,

some say Ho-ly Ghost, but I love to call you Friend. _____

WORDS: Helena Barrington
MUSIC: Helena Barrington, transcribed by William S. Moon

Your Power

"But you will receive power when the Holy Spirit has come upon you." (Acts 1:8a)

Moderately (♩ = 104)

1. _ You made _ me for your glo - ry, you plant -
(2. See there is) _____ a roam - ing li - on, who roars _

ed ev - er - y seed, _ they are grow - ing in - to sto -
_ to make me fear, _ to re - mind _ me of my fail -

WORDS: Brian C. Wilson and Leon Lewis
MUSIC: Brian C. Wilson and Leon Lewis, transcribed by William S. Moon

Holy Spirit Medley
80
Holy Spirit

"But you will receive power when the Holy Spirit has come upon you." (Acts 1:8a)

WORDS: Richard Smallwood
MUSIC: Richard Smallwood, arr. by Nolan Williams, Jr.

81

Let Your Spirit Come

"In the last days it will be, God declares,
that I will pour out my Spirit upon all flesh." (Acts 2:17a)

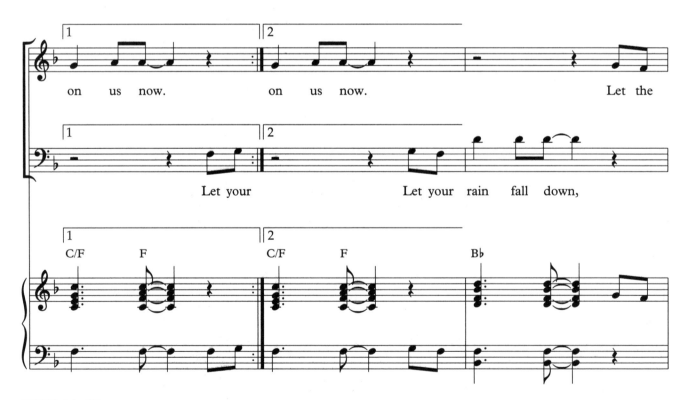

WORDS: John Chisum
MUSIC: John Chisum

© 1989 Ariose Music (ASCAP), admin. by EMI CMG Publishing

The Presence of the Lord Is Here

Tremble, O earth, at the presence of the LORD, at the presence of the God of Jacob. (Psalm 114:7)

1. The pres-ence of the Lord is here, the pres-ence of the Lord is
(2. The) spir - it of the Lord is here, the spir - it of the Lord is
(3. The) pow - er of the Lord is here, the pow - er of the Lord is

here. I feel it in the at - mos - phere, the pres-ence of the Lord is
here. I feel it in the at - mos - phere, the spir - it of the Lord is
here. I feel it in the at - mos - phere, the pow - er of the Lord is

here, the pres-ence of the Lord ____ is here. 2. The
here, the spir - it of the Lord ____ is here. 3. The
here, the pow - er of the Lord ____ is

*Omit if not performing medley.

WORDS: Kurt Carr
MUSIC: Kurt Carr

here!   Ev - ery - bod - y blow the trum - pet   and sound the a - larm.

Be - cause the Lord is in the tem - ple   let

ev - ery - bod - y bow.   Let

all the peo - ple praise him now, the Lord _____ is here!

End of **Holy Spirit Medley**

Praise God, from Whom All Blessings Flow

Praise the LORD! How good it is to sing praise to our God; for he is gracious. (Psalm 147:1)

WORDS: Thomas Ken, adapt. Isaac Watts and William Kethe
MUSIC: Adapt. John Hatton, by George Coles, arr. by Roberta Martin

Give Me Jesus

For to me, living is Christ and dying is gain. (Galatians 1:21)

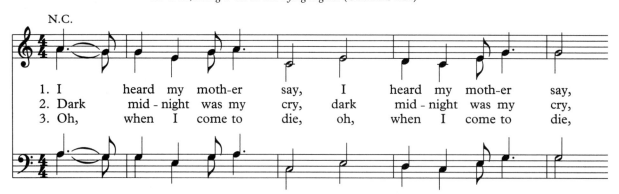

1. I heard my moth-er say, I heard my moth-er say,
2. Dark mid-night was my cry, dark mid-night was my cry,
3. Oh, when I come to die, oh, when I come to die,

I heard my moth-er say, "Give me Je - sus."
dark mid-night was my cry, give me Je - sus.
oh, when I come to die, give me Je - sus.

Refrain

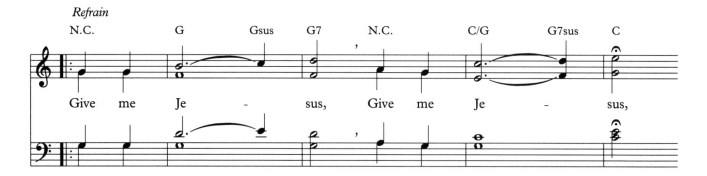

Give me Je - sus, Give me Je - sus,

you may have all this world, give me Je - sus.

WORDS: Traditional
MUSIC: Traditional, arr. by Verolga Nix

Harm. © 1981 Abingdon Press, admin. by The Copyright Co.

The Glory of His Presence Medley
Oh, the Glory of His Presence

Then the cloud covered the tent of meeting,
and the glory of the LORD filled the tabernacle. (Exodus 40:34)

Moderately slow (♩ = 80)

Oh, the glo - ry _____ of his pres - ence, _____

___ we your tem - ple _____ give him rev - erence. _____

WORDS: Steve Fry
MUSIC: Steve Fry

© 1983 BMG Songs/Birdwing Music (ASCAP), admin. by EMI CMG Publishing

The Glory of the Lord

86

And I looked, and lo! the glory of the LORD filled the temple of the LORD. (Ezekiel 44:4b)

WORDS: Gloria Gaither, William Gaither, and Richard Smallwood
MUSIC: Gloria Gaither, William Gaither, and Richard Smallwood, arr. by Nolan Williams, Jr.

Anointing

The anointing that you received from him abides in you, and so … abide in him. (1 John 2:27)

WORDS: Donn C. Thomas
MUSIC: Donn C. Thomas, arr. by Evelyn Simpson-Curenton

End of **The Glory of His Presence Medley**

To Every Generation

Lord, you have been our dwelling place in all generations. (Psalm 90:1)

WORDS: Bill Batstone and Cynthia Wilson
MUSIC: Bill Batstone, arr. by William S. Moon

89

Koinonia

The commandment we have from him is this:
those who love God must love their brothers and sisters also. (1 John 4:21)

WORDS: Michael McKay
MUSIC: Michael McKay, arr. by William S. Moon

90

Dwell in Unity

How very good and pleasant it is when kindred live together in unity! (Psalm 133:1)

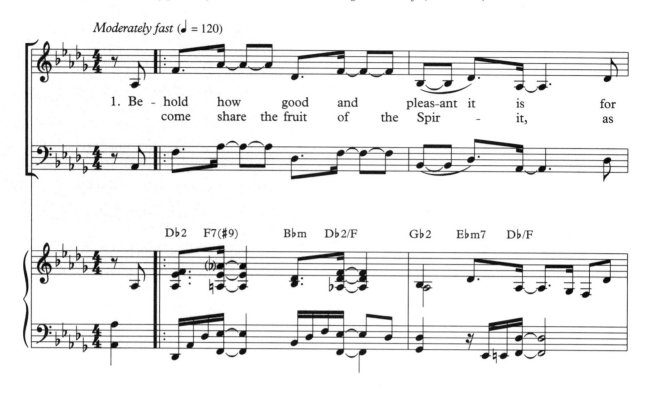

WORDS: Pamela Jean Davis
MUSIC: Pamela Jean Davis, transcribed by Keith Hampton, arr. by Mark A. Miller

DWELL IN UNITY
Irregular

Who Is My Mother, Who Is My Brother

*"Here are my mother and my brothers! Whoever does the will of God
is my brother and sister and mother." (Mark 3:34b)*

1. Who is my moth - er, who is my broth - er?
2. Dif - fer - ent - ly a - bled, dif - fer - ent - ly la - beled
3. Love will re - late us — col - or or sta - tus
4. Bound by one vi - sion, met for one mis - sion

All those who gath - er round Je - sus Christ:
wid - en the cir - cle round Je - sus Christ:
can't se - gre - gate us, round Je - sus Christ:
we claim each oth - er, round Je - sus Christ:

Spir - it - blown peo - ple, born from the Gos - pel
Crutch - es and stig - mas, cul - tures' e - nig - mas
Fam - i - ly fail - ings, hu - man de - rail - ings —
Here is my moth - er, here is my broth - er,

sit at the ta - ble, round Je - sus Christ.
all come to - geth - er, round Je - sus Christ.
all are ac - cept - ed, round Je - sus Christ.
kin - dred in Spir - it, through Je - sus Christ.

WORDS: Shirley Erena Murray
MUSIC: Jack Schrader
© 1992 Hope Publishing Co.

KINDRED
54.54 D

92

There's No Me, There's No You

So we, who are many, are one body in Christ,
and individually we are members one of another. (Romans 12:5)

WORDS: Evelyn Reynolds, adapt. by Nolan Williams, Jr.
MUSIC: Evelyn Reynolds, arr. by Nolan Williams, Jr.

Adapt. and arr. © 2000 GIA Publications, Inc.

Make Us One

"The glory that you have given me I have given them,
so that they may be one, as we are one." (John 17:22)

MAKE US ONE
Irregular

94

Step
(For Ushers)

I would rather be a doorkeeper in the house of my God
than live in the tents of wickedness. (Psalm 84:10b)

Not too fast ($\downarrow$ = 76)

N.C.

B♭7   Fm11/A♭   B♭7   A♭13

Group 1   Group 2   Group 1   Group 2   All

Step,   step,   step,   step,   step in-to the house of the Lord. _

B♭7   Fm11/A♭   B♭7   A♭13

Group 1   Group 2   Group 1   Group 2   All   *Fine*

Step,   step,   step,   step,   step in-to the pres-ence of God. _

B♭7   Fm11/A♭   B♭7   A♭13   *Fine*

See Performance Notes.

WORDS: Gennifer Benjamin Brooks
MUSIC: Marilyn E. Thornton

Rule of Life

Show me your faith apart from your works,
and I by my works will show you my faith. (James 2:18b)

WORDS: And 18th cent. aphorism, attr. to John Wesley
MUSIC: Edward Bonnemere, arr. by Cynthia Wilson

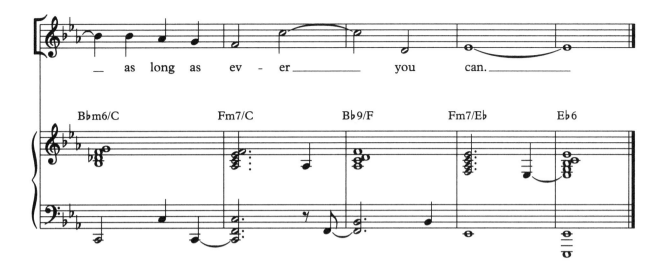

Affirmation

96

Jesus said to him, "No one who puts a hand to the plow and looks back
is fit for the kingdom of God." (Luke 9:62)

Very fast (♩ = 168)

1. I will fol - low in God's name _ when Je - sus calls to me.
2. I will o - pen up my heart _ to ev - ery - one in need.
3. I will o - pen up my hands _ to do your Ho - ly will.
4. I will com - fort with your love _ in ev - ery hid - den place,
5. Let us gath - er in your name _ and lift our hands in praise.

Add percussion with a Caribbean feel, as desired.

WORDS: Marilyn E. Thornton
MUSIC: Marilyn E. Thornton

I will trust you just the same _ wher-ev - er I may be.
I will move to do my part _ for shac-kles to be freed.
I will give up ev - ery plan, _ your pur-pose to ful - fill.
with your Spir - it from a - bove _ so they may know your grace.
You will break off ev - ery chain _ and val - leys you will raise.

I will seek your will to do; _ I will tell the gos - pel news. _
Ev - ery ac - tion, ev - ery word, _ ev - ery part of me will serve. _
For the peo - ple far and near, _ I will show them that we care; _
Man - y blind - ed souls will see, _ and the truth will set them free. _
I will sing from moun-tains high. _ I will fol - low till I die. _

How Like a Gentle Spirit

By the tender mercy of our God the dawn from on high will break upon us…
to guide our feet into the way of peace. (Luke 1:78-79)

Prayerfully, with the feel of a spiritual.

WORDS: C. Eric Lincoln
MUSIC: Mark A. Miller

BALTIMORE
10.10.10.10

He Who Began a Good Work in You

I am confident of this, that the one who began a good work among you
will bring it to completion by the day of Jesus Christ. (Philippians 1:6)

WORDS: Jon Mohr
MUSIC: Jon Mohr

A GOOD WORK
Irregular

ful to com-plete it. _____ He who start - ed the work will be faith - ful to com-plete it in you. _

To repeat   To end

To repeat   To end

99

We All Are One in Mission

Now there are varieties of gifts, but the same Spirit; and there are
varieties of services, but the same Lord. (1 Corinthians 12:4-5)

1. We all are one in mis - sion, we all are one in call, _____
2. We all are called for ser - vice, to wit-ness in God's name. _
3. Now let us be u - nit - ed, and let our song be heard. _

WORDS: Rusty Edwards
MUSIC: Marilyn E. Thornton, arr. by Mark A. Miller

100

Grace Alone

For by grace you have been saved through faith,
and this is not your own doing; it is the gift of God. (Ephesians 2:8)

With movement

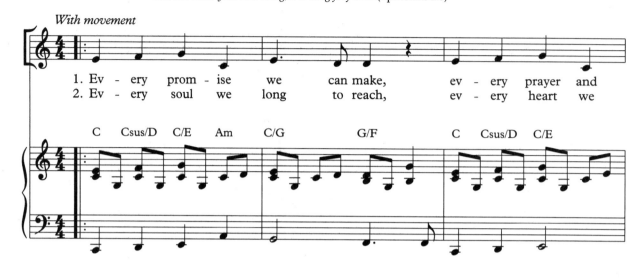

1. Ev – ery prom – ise we can make, ev – ery prayer and
2. Ev – ery soul we long to reach, ev – ery heart we

step of faith, ev – ery dif – ference we will make
hope to teach, ev – ery – where we share his peace

is on – ly by his grace. Ev – ery moun – tain
is on – ly by his grace. Ev – ery lov – ing

WORDS: Scott Wesley Brown and Jeff Nelson
MUSIC: Scott Wesley Brown and Jeff Nelson
© 1998 Maranatha! Music, admin. by Music Services

GRACE ALONE
Irregular with Refrain

253

I Give All to You

She out of her poverty has put in all she had to live on. (Luke 21:4b)

1. I give all my ser-vice to you, I give
2. I give all my prob-lems to you, I give
3. I give all my fam-ily to you, I give
4. I give all my fu-ture to you, I give
5. I give all my wor-ship to you, I give

all my ser-vice to you; no mat-ter the cost or
all my prob-lems to you; no mat-ter the cost or
all my fam-ily to you; no mat-ter the cost or
all my fu-ture to you; no mat-ter the cost or
all my wor-ship to you; no mat-ter the cost or

WORDS: Larnelle Harris
MUSIC: Larnelle Harris, arr. by William S. Moon
© 1987 Life Song Music Press

what oth - ers do,   I give all   my ser - vice to you.
what oth - ers do,   I give all   my prob-lems to you.
what oth - ers do,   I give all   my fam - ily to you.
what oth - ers do,   I give all   my fu - ture to you.
what oth - ers do,   I give all   my wor-ship to you.

World Without Walls

What is the house that you would build for me, and what is my resting place? (Isaiah 66:1b)

1. Place my
(2. With God's)
(3. Quick - ly)
(4. Help the)
(5. Ev - ery) -

feet on the land where no bar - ri - ers stand and its
grace from a - bove fill each heart with such love that we
sound through the din o - ver col - or of skin, though the
young work with old, and the rich share their gold; make our
one on this earth is our neigh - bor by birth, and our

WORDS: David A. Robb and Amanda Husberg
MUSIC: Newlove Annan

Words © 2005 Wayne Leupold Editions, Inc.; music © 2007 Abingdon Press, admin. by The Copyright Co.

This music comes in the musical (rhythmic) style called the "Hi Life." Hi Life Music or rhythm, was created in the western part of Africa. It is basically a fusion of Caribbean, West and Central African indigenous rhythms, such as Calypso, Samba, Kwasa, and Kpanlogo. It is a danceable rhythm.

103 There's a Spirit of Love in This Place

Above all, clothe yourselves with love,
which binds everything together in perfect harmony. (Colossians 3:14)

1. There's a spir-it of love in this place, there's a spir-it of love in this place. You can't see it, but it's there, just as pre-cious as the air. There's a spir-it of love in this
(2. There's the) pres-ence of peace in this room, there's the pres-ence of peace in this room. In God's ten-der-ness is found peace that pass-es hu-man bounds. There's the pres-ence of peace in this

WORDS: Mark A. Miller
MUSIC: Mark A. Miller

MEDEMA
Irregular

Ain't Gonna Let Nobody
Turn Me 'Round*

*I press on toward the goal for the prize
of the heavenly call of God in Christ Jesus.* (Philippians 3:14)

**Change this word only for each new verse.

2. segregation
3. persecution
4. hatred
5. jail house
6. police dogs
7. billy club (night stick)
8. fire hose
9. tear gas

WORDS: African American spiritual
MUSIC: African American spiritual, arr. by Lavinia L. T. Odejimi

*This song, like many others, was adapted from a historical
spiritual to meet the needs of the Civil Rights Movement.

Original words:

    Don't you let nobody turn you 'round, turn you 'round, turn you 'round,
    Don't you let nobody turn you 'round, you gotta keep on a-walkin',
    Keep on a-talkin', marchin' on to Canaan land.

105

Woke Up This Morning

But I will sing of your might;
I will sing aloud of your steadfast love in the morning. (Psalm 59:16a)

1. Woke up this morn-ing with my mind   stayed on Je - sus.
2. Woke up this morn-ing with my mind   stayed on free - dom.
3. Walk - in' and talk - in' with my mind   stayed on free - dom.
4. Can't hate your neigh-bor with your mind   stayed on free - dom.

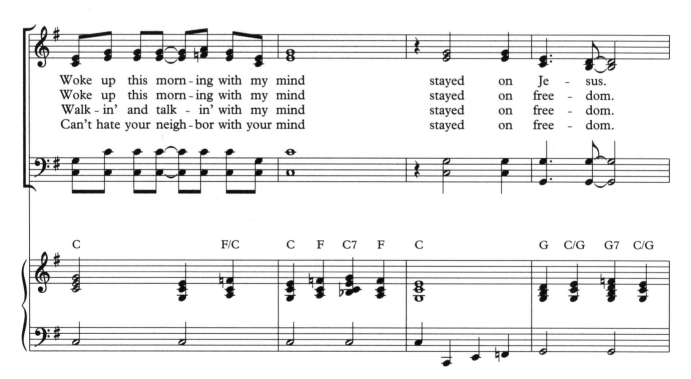

Woke up this morn-ing with my mind   stayed on Je - sus.
Woke up this morn-ing with my mind   stayed on free - dom.
Walk - in' and talk - in' with my mind   stayed on free - dom.
Can't hate your neigh-bor with your mind   stayed on free - dom.

WORDS: African American spiritual
MUSIC: African American spiritual, arr. by Marilyn E. Thornton

WOKE UP THIS MORNING
Irregular

Woke up this morn - ing with my mind
Woke up this morn - ing with my mind
Walk - in' and talk - in' with my mind
Can't hate your neigh - bor with your mind

Ooo
Ooo

stayed on Je - sus.
stayed on free - dom.
stayed on free - dom. Hal - le -
stayed on free - dom.

lu, hal - le - lu, hal - le - lu - jah! jah!

Hal - le - lu, hal - le - lu, hal - le - lu - jah! jah!

106   We Shall Overcome

Who is it that conquers the world
but the one who believes that Jesus is the Son of God? (1 John 5:5)

Inspired by African American Gospel Singing, members of the Food & Tobacco Workers Union, Charleston, South Carolina, and the southern Civil Rights Movement. Royalties derived from this composition are being contributed to the We Shall Overcome Fund and The Freedom Movement under the Trusteeship of the writers.

WORDS: Trad., adapt. by Zilphia Horton, Frank Hamilton, Guy Carawan, and Pete Seeger
MUSIC: Trad., adapt. by Zilphia Horton, Frank Hamilton, Guy Carawan, and Pete Seeger,
    arr. by Monya Davis Logan

MARTIN
Irregular

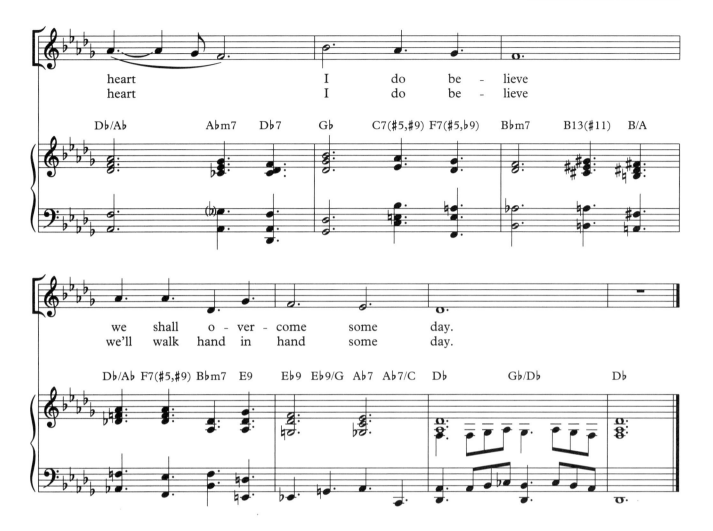

heart   I do be - lieve

we shall o - ver - come some day.
we'll walk hand in hand some day.

Freedom Afterwhile

107

Neither shall they learn war anymore…and no one shall make them afraid. (Micah 4:3b, 4b)

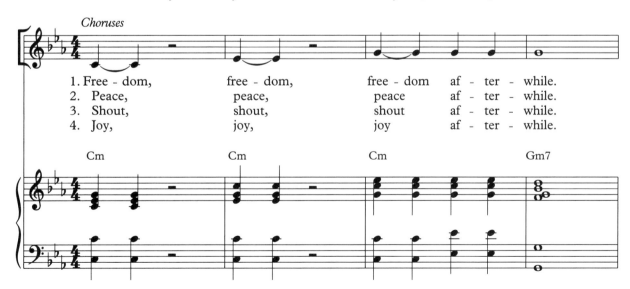

1. Free - dom, free - dom, free - dom af - ter - while.
2. Peace, peace, peace af - ter - while.
3. Shout, shout, shout af - ter - while.
4. Joy, joy, joy af - ter - while.

WORDS: Michael L. Charles
MUSIC: Michael L. Charles

Freedom, / freedom, / freedom afterwhile.
Peace, / peace, / peace afterwhile.
Shout, / shout, / shout afterwhile.
Joy, / joy, / joy afterwhile.

1. One day this war will be over, we'll lay our armor down.
2. This world is full of sorrow, crying on every hand.

Walk on up the King's highway, and get our starry crown.
God's gonna wipe all tears away, and lead us to the promised land.

Spiritual Medley for Pentecost

108

*But those who wait on the LORD shall renew their strength, they shall mount up with wings
like eagles, they shall run and not be weary, they shall walk and not faint. (Isaiah 40:31)*

WORDS: Trad. African American
MUSIC: Trad. African American, arr. by Cynthia Wilson
© 2007 Cynthia Wilson

val - ley in peace. _____ When we

dren, don't you get wea - ry. When we

tram - pin', tryin' to make heab - 'n my home. When we

_ it by him - self. When we

Em7/A   D7   C   G/B   Am7 G   D

SA

all _____ get to heav - en, ___ what a

G   G7   C   C/D F#m7(♭5) G   G   F#dim7/E♭

Freedom Medley
O Freedom

The small and the great are there, and the slaves are free from their masters. (Job 3:19)

109

WORDS: African American spiritual
MUSIC: African American spiritual, arr. by William S. Moon

Freedom Is Coming

So if the Son makes you free, you will be free indeed. (John 8:36)

*Omit notes in pickup measure if not performing as part of medley.

**Parts for claves, bongos, and conga or tom tom are printed after this song.

WORDS: Trad. South African
MUSIC: Trad. South African

© 1984 Utryck, admin. by Walton Music Group

End of **Freedom Medley**

Freedom Is Coming

($\quarternote$ = 160)

MUSIC: Trad. South African

© 1984 Utryck, admin. by Walton Music Group

111

We Are Singing
(Siyahamba/Caminando)

But now in the Lord, you are light. Live as children of light. (Ephesians 5:8b)

(English) We are sing - ing* in the light of God, we are
(Zulu**) Si - ya - hamb' e - ku - kha - nyen' kwen - khos', si - ya -
(Spanish) Ca - mi - nan - do en la luz de Dios, ca - mi -

sing - ing in the light of God. ___ We are
hamb' e - ku - kha - nyen' kwen - khos. ___ Si - ya -
nan - do en la luz de Dios. ___ Ca - mi -

*walking, ringing, marching, dancing, praying, etc.

WORDS: South Africa (20th cent.)
MUSIC: South Africa (20th cent.)

SIYAHAMBA
Irregular

© 1984 Utryck, used by permission of Walton Music Corp.

112

We Are Real People

"He has sent me to proclaim release to the captives…to let the oppressed go free." (Luke 4:18b)

WORDS: Donn Thomas
MUSIC: Donn Thomas

113

Lift Every Voice and Sing

Be filled with the Spirit, as you sing psalms and hymns
and spiritual songs…giving thanks to God. (Ephesians 5:18b-20a)

1. Lift ev-ery voice and sing, till earth and heav - en ring,
2. Ston - y the road we trod, bit - ter the chas - tening rod,
3. God of our wea - ry years, God of our si - lent tears,

ring with the har - mo - nies of lib - er - ty;
felt in the days when hope un - born had died;
thou who hast brought us thus far on the way;

let our re - joic - ing rise, high as the lis - tening skies,
yet with a stead - y beat, have not our wea - ry feet,
thou who hast by thy might, led us in - to the light,

let it re - sound loud as the roll - ing sea.
come to the place for which our fa - thers sighed?
keep us for - ev - er in the path, we pray.

WORDS: James Weldon Johnson
MUSIC: J. Rosamond Johnson
© 1921 Edward B. Marks Music Co.

LIFT EVERY VOICE
Irregular

114

There Is a Balm

Is there no balm in Gilead? Is there no physician there? (Jeremiah 8:22a)

There is a balm in Gil-e-ad, to make the wound-ed whole; ____

— there is a balm in Gil-e-ad, to heal the sin-sick soul.

WORDS: African American spiritual
MUSIC: African American spiritual, arr. by William S. Moon
Arr. © 2007 Abingdon Press, admin. by The Copyright Co.

BALM IN GILEAD
Irregular

1. Some-times I feel dis-cour-aged, and think my work's in vain, but
2. If you can't preach like Pe-ter, if you can't pray like Paul, just

then the Ho-ly Spir-it re-vives my soul a-gain. _____ There is a
tell the love of Je-sus, and say he died for all. _____ There is a

D.S. al Fine

I Will Restore

115

For I will restore health to you, and your wounds I will heal. (Jeremiah 30:17a)

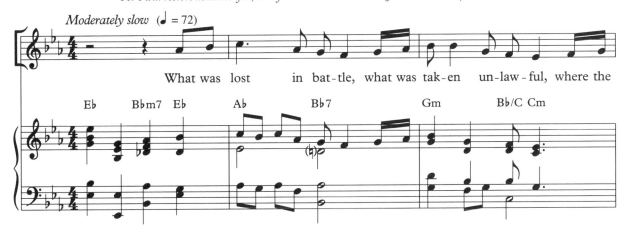

What was lost in bat-tle, what was tak-en un-law-ful, where the

WORDS: Richard Johnson
MUSIC: Richard Johnson, arr. by William S. Moon

store to you all of this and more. I will re-store to you all of this and more.

Give Me a Clean Heart

116

Create in me a clean heart, O God, and put a new and right spirit within me. (Psalm 51:10)

Very slowly (♩. = 40)

Refrain

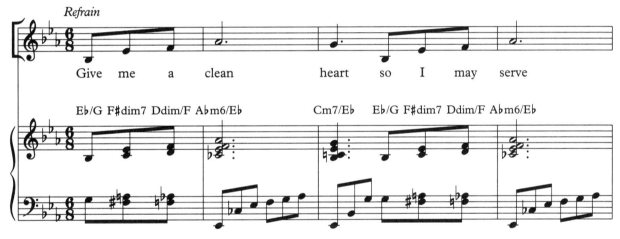

Give me a clean heart so I may serve

thee, Lord, fix my heart so that I may be used by

WORDS: Margaret Pleasant Douroux
MUSIC: Margaret Pleasant Douroux, arr. by Albert Dennis Tessier

DOUROUX
Irregular

117

Glory, Glory, Hallelujah!

"I relieved your shoulder of the burden; your hands were freed from the basket." (Psalm 81:6)

WORDS: Trad.
MUSIC: Trad., arr. by Mark A. Miller
Arr. © 2007 Abingdon Press, admin. by The Copyright Co.

GLORY
15 15

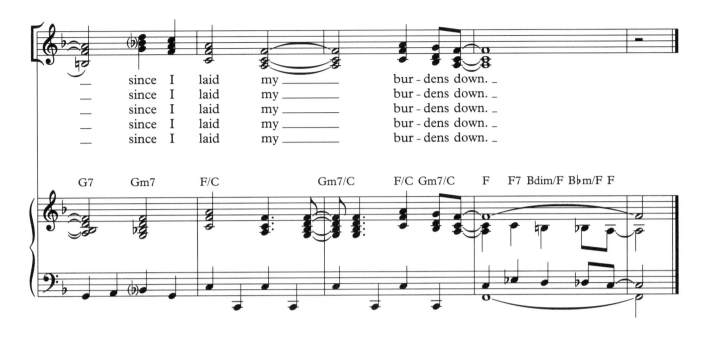

since I laid my _____ bur-dens down. _
since I laid my _____ bur-dens down. _
since I laid my _____ bur-dens down. _
since I laid my _____ bur-dens down. _
since I laid my _____ bur-dens down. _

G7 Gm7 F/C Gm7/C F/C Gm7/C F F7 Bdim/F Bbm/F F

Come On in My Room

118

Then he put them all outside, and took the child's father and mother and those who
were with him, and went in where the child was. (Mark 5:40)

(♩. = 60 *or slower*)

1. Come on in ma room. Oh,
2. Joy in ma room. Oh,
3. Peace in ma room. Oh,
4. Heal-ing in ma room. Oh,

C   F   C   E/G#

*To be sung in an improvisory manner, with liberty. See Performance Notes.

WORDS: African American traditional
MUSIC: African American traditional, arr. by Cecilia L. Clemons

Heal Me

They laid the sick in the marketplaces, and begged him that they might touch
even the fringe of his cloak; and all who touched it were healed. (Mark 6:56*b*)

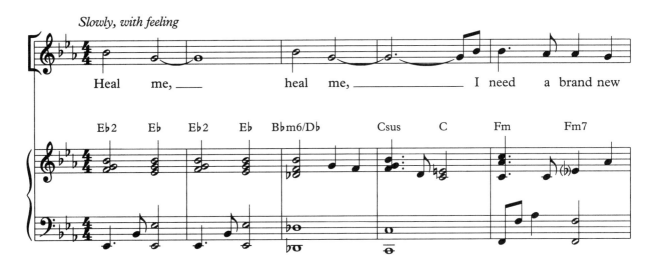

Heal me, ____ heal me, _____ I need a brand new

touch from you, my Lord; _____ heal me, ____

heal me, ____ let the full - ness of your life now be re - stored. ____

WORDS: Terry MacAlmon
MUSIC: Terry MacAlmon

Father, I Stretch My Hands to Thee

I stretch out my hands to you; my soul thirsts for you like a parched land. (Psalm 143:6)

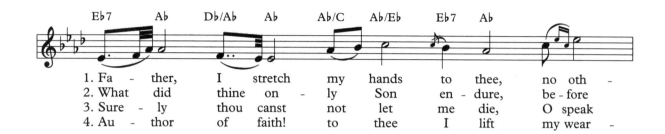

1. Fa - ther, I stretch my hands to thee, no oth -
2. What did thine on - ly Son en - dure, be - fore
3. Sure - ly thou canst not let me die, O speak
4. Au - thor of faith! to thee I lift my wear -

er help I know; if thou with - draw thy - self
I drew my breath! What pain, what la - bor to
and I shall live; and here I will un - wear -
y, long - ing eyes; O let me now re - ceive

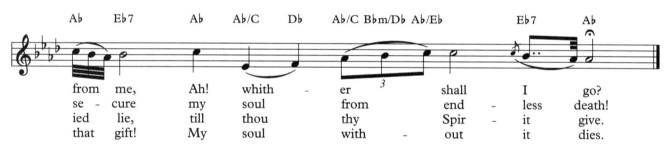

from me, Ah! whith - er shall I go?
se - cure my soul from end - less death!
ied lie, till thou thy Spir - it give.
that gift! My soul with - out it dies.

See Performance Notes.

WORDS: Charles Wesley
MUSIC: Hugh Wilson, lined by J. Jefferson Cleveland and Verolga Nix

MARTYRDOM
CM

Higher, Higher

For your steadfast love is higher than the heavens,
and your faithfulness reaches to the clouds. (Psalm 108:4)

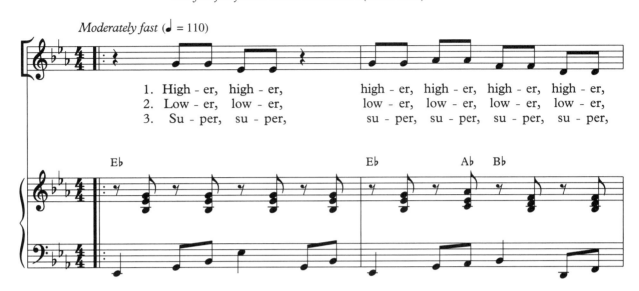

1. High - er, high - er, high - er, high - er, high - er, high - er,
2. Low - er, low - er, low - er, low - er, low - er, low - er,
3. Su - per, su - per, su - per, su - per, su - per, su - per,

high-er, high-er.   **1, 2** Lift Je - sus high-er!
low-er, low-er.   Stomp the dev - il low-er!
su-per, su-per.   **3** Su-per-nat - u-ral pow-er!

See Performance Notes.

WORDS: Anonymous
MUSIC: Anonymous, arr. by Nolan Williams, Jr.

122

Come and Go with Me

"Come, let us go up to the mountain of the LORD, to the house of the God of Jacob;
that he may teach us his ways and that we may walk in his paths." (Micah 4:2)

1. Come and go with me to my Fa-ther's house,
2. Come and go with me to my Fa-ther's house,
3. Come and go with me to my Fa-ther's house,

to my Fa - ther's house to my Fa - ther's house.
to my Fa - ther's house to my Fa - ther's house.
to my Fa - ther's house to my Fa - ther's house.

WORDS: Trad. African American
MUSIC: Trad. African American, arr. by Marilyn E. Thornton

COME AND GO WITH ME
10 10 10 5

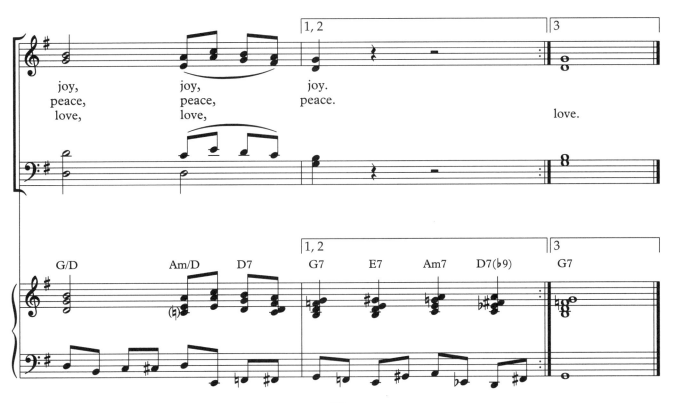

123

Victory Is Mine

But thanks be to God, who gives us the victory through our Lord Jesus Christ. (1 Corinthians 15:57)

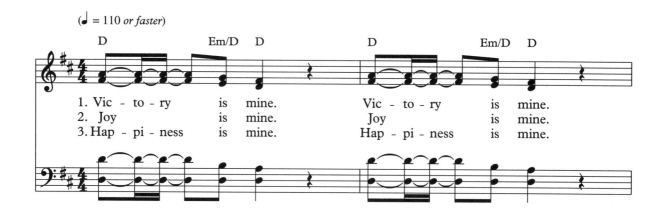

1. Vic - to - ry is mine. Vic - to - ry is mine.
2. Joy is mine. Joy is mine.
3. Hap - pi - ness is mine. Hap - pi - ness is mine.

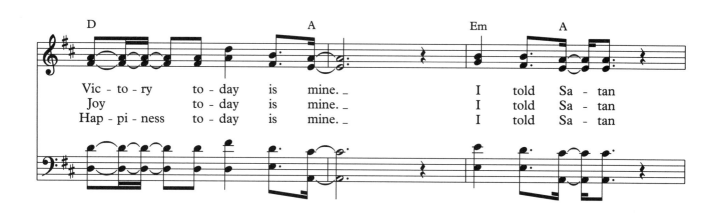

Vic - to - ry to - day is mine. _ I told Sa - tan
Joy to - day is mine. _ I told Sa - tan
Hap - pi - ness to - day is mine. _ I told Sa - tan

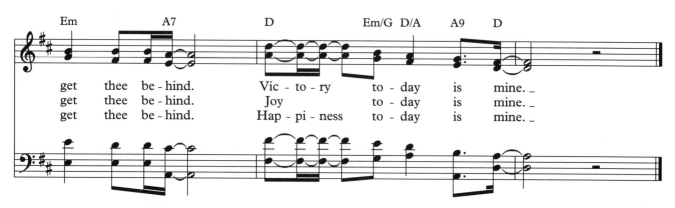

get thee be - hind. Vic - to - ry to - day is mine. _
get thee be - hind. Joy to - day is mine. _
get thee be - hind. Hap - pi - ness to - day is mine. _

WORDS: Dorothy Norwood and Alvin Darling
MUSIC: Dorothy Norwood and Alvin Darling, arr. by Stephen Key

VICTORY
55787

I Thank You, Jesus

124

He prostrated himself at Jesus' feet and thanked him. And he was a Samaritan. (Luke 17:16)

Moderately (♩. = 100)

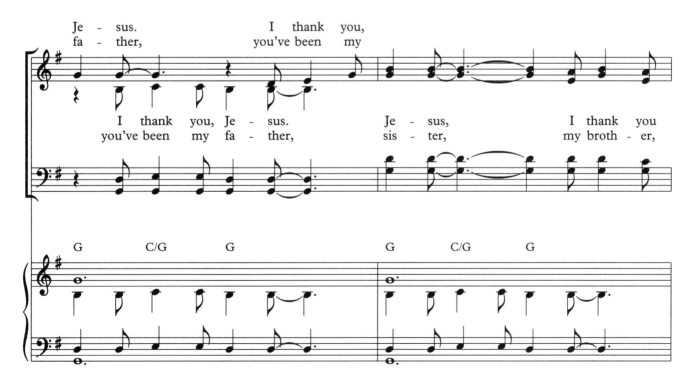

WORDS: Kenneth Morris
MUSIC: Kenneth Morris, arr. by Joseph Joubert

125

The Lord Is Blessing Me Right Now

Blessed be the God and Father of our Lord Jesus Christ,
who has blessed us in Christ with every spiritual blessing. (Ephesians 1:3)

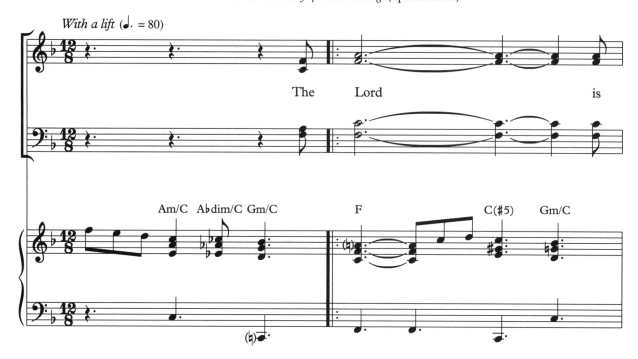

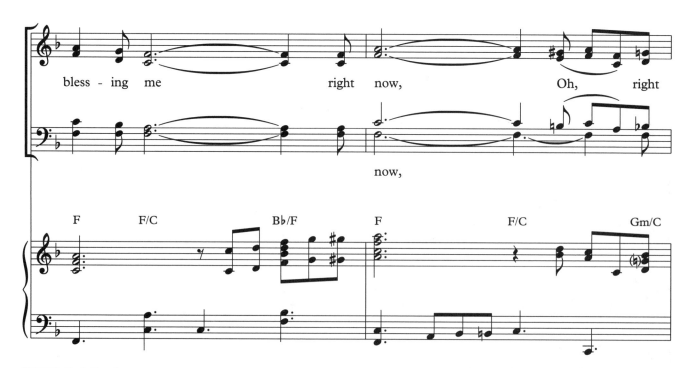

WORDS: Trad. Gospel
MUSIC: Trad. Gospel, arr. by Nolan Williams, Jr.

I Remember

Remember me, O LORD, when you show favor to your people; …
that I may glory in your heritage. (Psalm 106:4-5)

See Performance Notes.

WORDS: Frederick Burchell and Craig Watkins
MUSIC: Frederick Burchell and Kyle Lovett

© 2007 B4 Entertainment

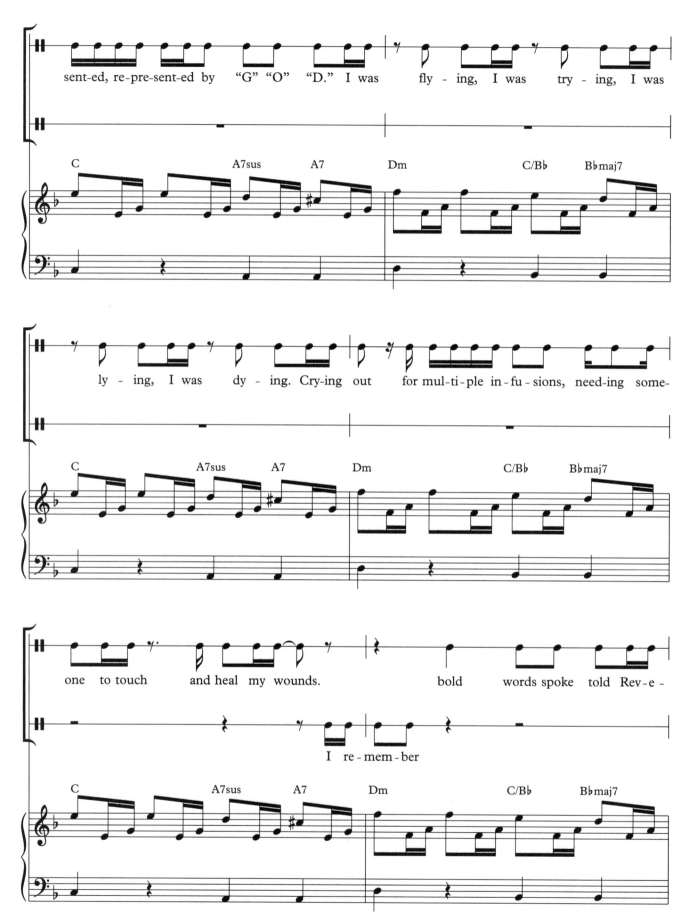

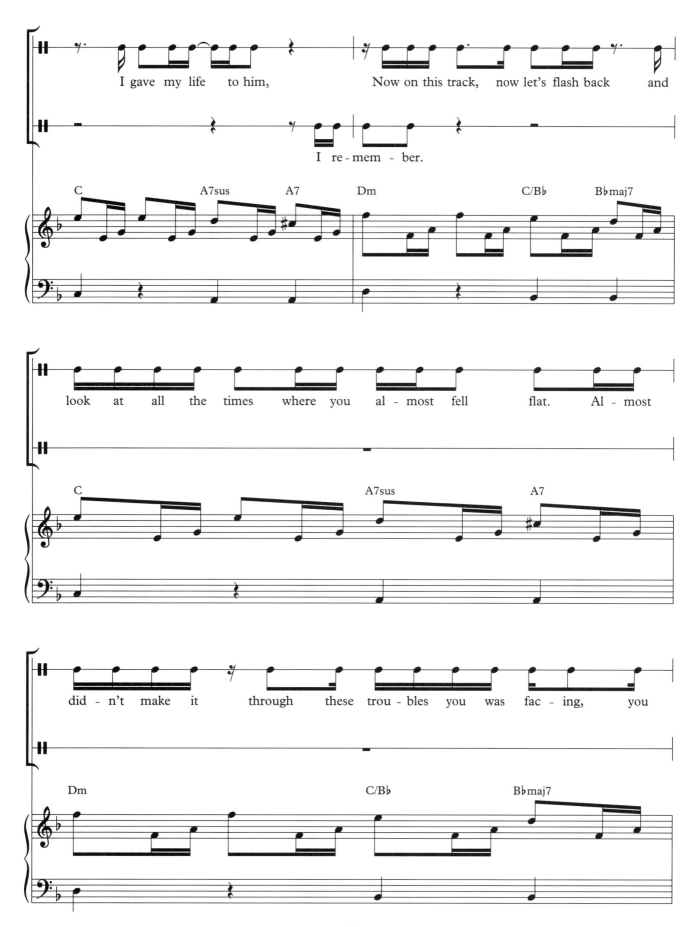

311

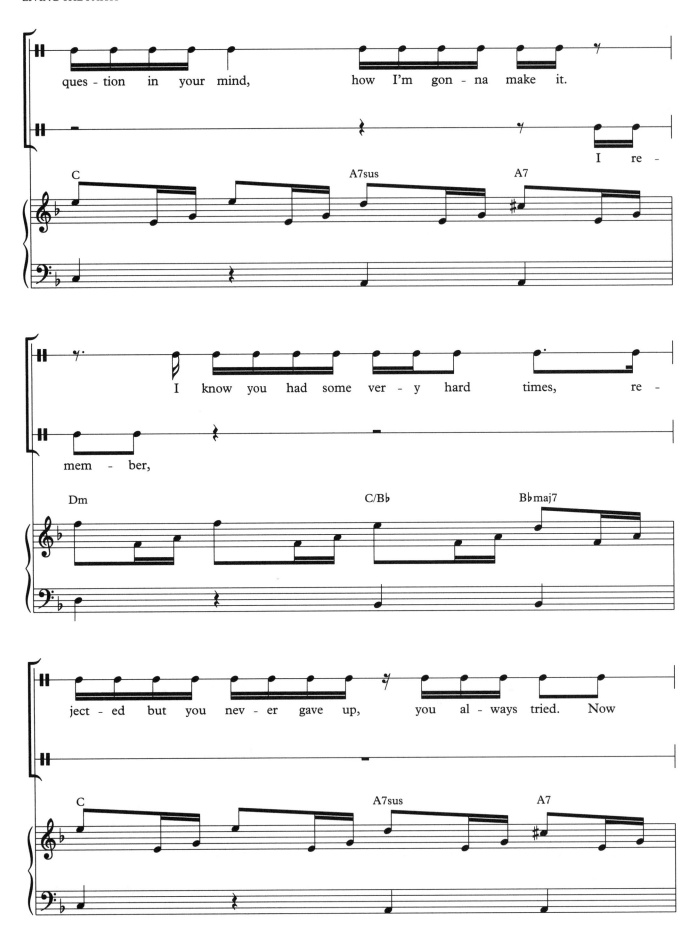

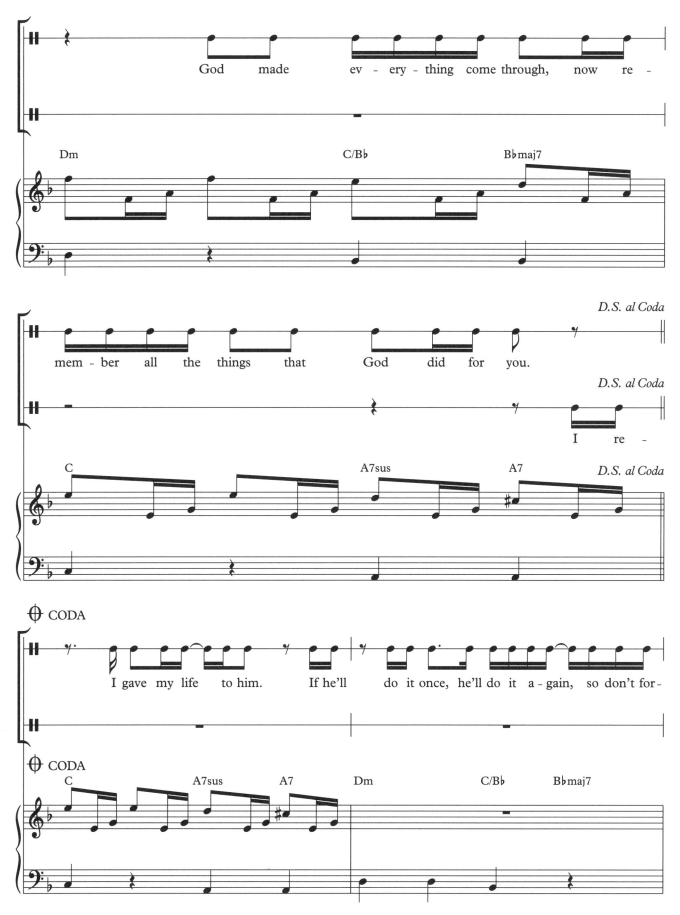

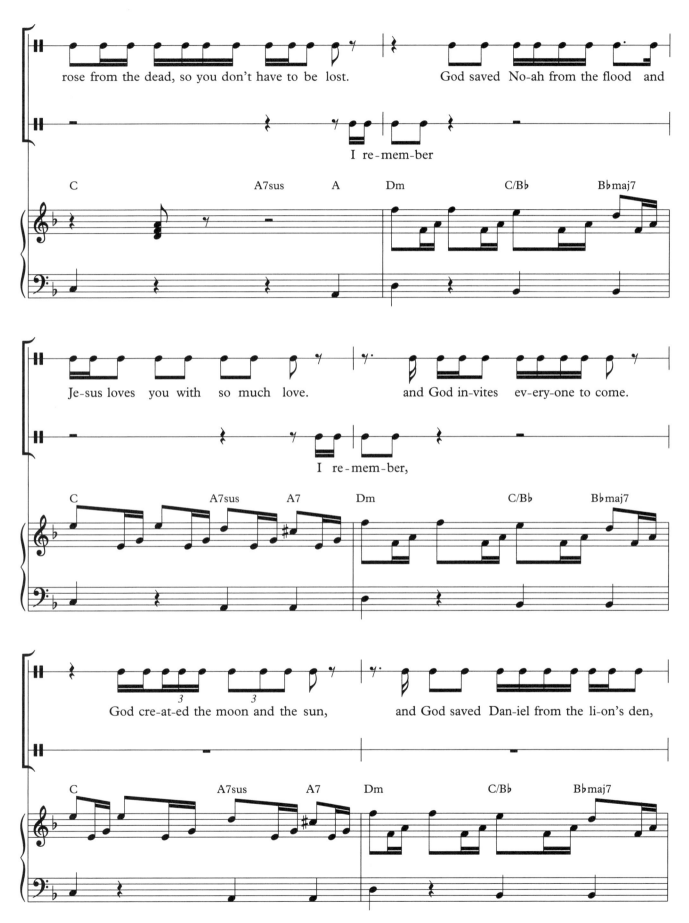

126

I Remember

Drum Set

MUSIC: Frederick Burchell and Kyle Lovett
© 2007 B4 Entertainment

Give Thanks

By him therefore let us offer the sacrifice of praise to God continually, that is,
the fruit of our lips giving thanks to his name. (Hebrews 13:15 KJV)

Give thanks with a grate-ful heart, give thanks to the

Ho-ly One, give thanks be-cause he's giv-en Je-sus Christ, his

Son. Give thanks with a grate-ful heart, give

WORDS: Henry Smith
MUSIC: Henry Smith, arr. by Oscar Dismuke

GIVE THANKS
Irregular

Your Grace and Mercy

But by the grace of God I am what I am,
and his grace toward me has not been in vain. (1 Corinthians 15:10)

WORDS: Franklin D. Williams
MUSIC: Franklin D. Williams, arr. by Nolan Williams, Jr.

© 1993 Malaco Music Co. (BMI)

D.S.

129 Watch Night

"Keep awake therefore, for you do not know on what day your Lord is coming." (Matthew 24:42)

WORDS: Gennifer Benjamin Brooks
MUSIC: Marilyn E. Thornton

130

The Right Hand of God

The right hand of the LORD is exalted; the right hand of the LORD does valiantly. (Psalm 118:16)

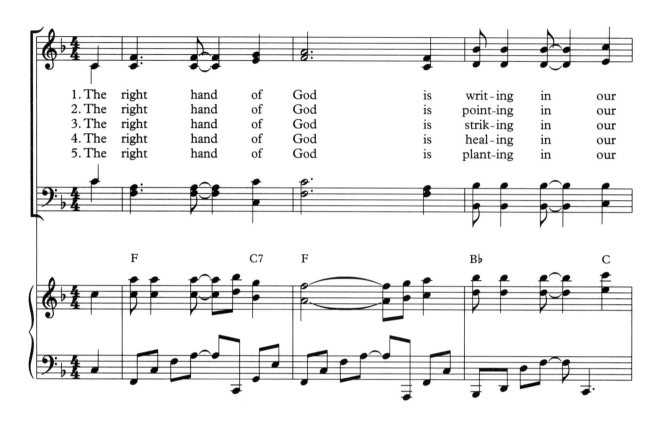

1. The right hand of God is writ-ing in our
2. The right hand of God is point-ing in our
3. The right hand of God is strik-ing in our
4. The right hand of God is heal-ing in our
5. The right hand of God is plant-ing in our

1. land, writ - ing with pow - er and with love, _____
2. land, point - ing the way we must go. _____
3. land, strik - ing out at en - vy, hate, and greed. _____
4. land, heal - ing bro - ken bod - ies, minds, and souls. _____
5. land, plant - ing seeds of free - dom, hope, and love. _____

WORDS: Patrick Prescod
MUSIC: Noel Dexter, piano arr. by Darryl Glenn Nettles

our   con - flicts   and   our   fears,   our   tri - umphs   and   our
So   cloud - ed   is   the   way,   so   eas - i - ly   we
Our   self - ish - ness   and   lust,   our   pride and   deeds   un -
So   won - drous   is   its   touch   with   love that   means   so
In   these Ca - rib - bean   lands,   let   his peo - ple   all   join

tears   are   re - cord - ed   by   the   right   hand   of   God.
stray,   but   we're   guid - ed   by   the   right   hand   of   God.
just,   are   de - stroyed   by   the   right   hand   of   God.
much,   when   we're   healed   by   the   right   hand   of   God.
hands   and   be   one   with   the   right   hand   of   God.

131
When We All Get to Heaven

We have a building from God, a house not made with hands,
eternal in the heavens. (2 Corinthians 5:1b)

WORDS: Eliza Edmunds Hewitt
MUSIC: Emily Divine Wilson, arr. by Regina Hoosier, transcribed by Marilyn E. Thornton
Arr. © 2007 Regina Hoosier

HEAVEN
87.87 with Refrain

The Jesus in Me

Let mutual love continue. (Hebrews 13:1)

WORDS: Anonymous
MUSIC: Anonymous, arr. by Cynthia Wilson
Arr. © 2007 Abingdon Press, admin. by The Copyright Co.

133

A Shield About Me

But you, O LORD, are a shield around me. (Psalm 3:3a)

WORDS: Donn Thomas and Charles Williams
MUSIC: Donn Thomas and Charles Williams, arr. by Willam S. Moon

134

God Is

God said to Moses, "I AM WHO I AM." (Exodus 3:14a)

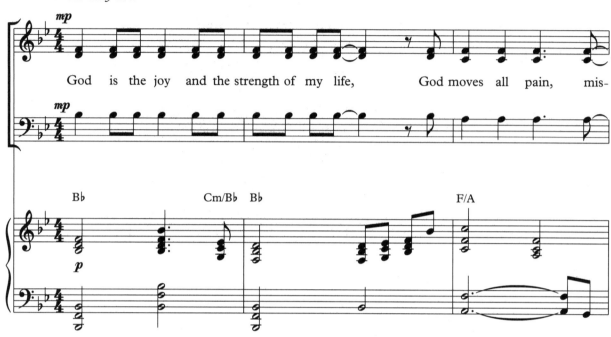

God is the joy and the strength of my life, God moves all pain, mis-

er - y, and strife, God prom-ised to keep me, nev-er to leave me, God's

WORDS: Dr. Robert J. Fryson
MUSIC: Dr. Robert J. Fryson, arr. by Mark A. Miller

Music © 1976 GIA Publications, Inc.; arr. © 2007 Abingdon Press, admin. by The Copyright Co.

GOD IS
Irr.

Goin' Up Yonder

For the perishable body must put on imperishability,
and this mortal body must put on immortality. (1 Corinthians 15:53)

WORDS: Walter Hawkins
MUSIC: Walter Hawkins, arr. by William S. Moon

136

Soon and Very Soon

"See, I am coming soon; my reward is with me,
to repay according to everyone's work." (Revelation 22:12)

WORDS: Andraé Crouch
MUSIC: Andraé Crouch, arr. by William S. Moon
© 1976 Crouch Music/Bud John Songs, Inc. (ASCAP), admin. by EMI CMG Publishing

VERY SOON
Irregular

137

O I Want to See Him

For now we see in a mirror dimly, but then we will see face to face. (1 Corinthians 13:12a)

Slowly, with a lilt (♩. = 76)

1. As I jour-ney through the land sing-ing as I go,
2. When in ser-vice for my Lord dark may be the night,
3. When in val-leys low I look toward the moun-tain height,
4. When be-fore me bil-lows rise from the might-y deep,

point-ing souls to Cal-va-ry — to the crim-son flow,
but I'll cling more close to him, he will give me light;
and be-hold my Sav-ior there, lead-ing in the fight,
then my Lord di-rects my bark; he doth safe-ly keep,

man-y ar-rows pierce my soul from with-out, with-in;
Sa-tan's snares may vex my soul, turn my thoughts a-side;
with a ten-der hand out-stretched toward the val-ley low,
and he leads me gen-tly on through this world be-low;

but my Lord leads me on, through him I must win.
but my Lord goes a-head, leads what-e'er be-tide.
guid-ing me I can see, as I on-ward go.
he's a real friend to me, O I love him so.

WORDS: Rufus H. Cornelius
MUSIC: Rufus H. Cornelius

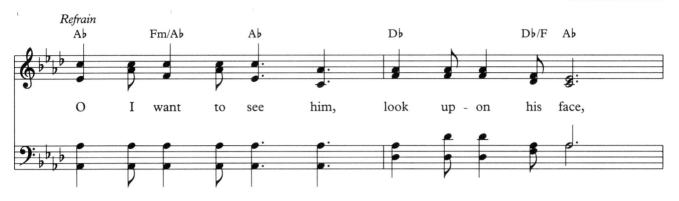

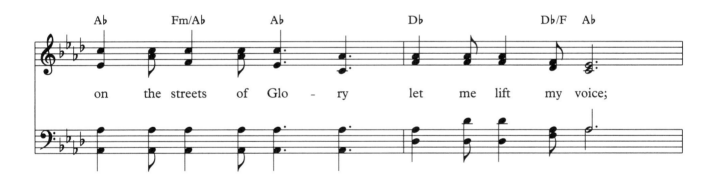

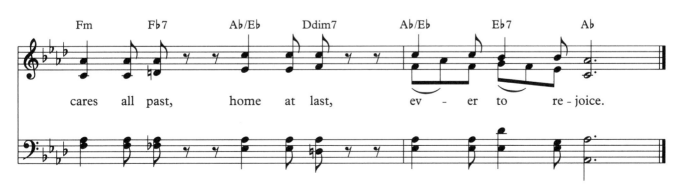

138
He'll Understand and Say "Well Done"

His lord said unto him, "Well done, good and faithful servant." (Matthew 25:23a KJV)

1. If when you give the best of your ser - vice,
2. Mis - un - der - stood, the Sav - ior of sin - ners,
3. If when this life of la - bor is end - ed,
4. But if you try and fail in your try - ing,

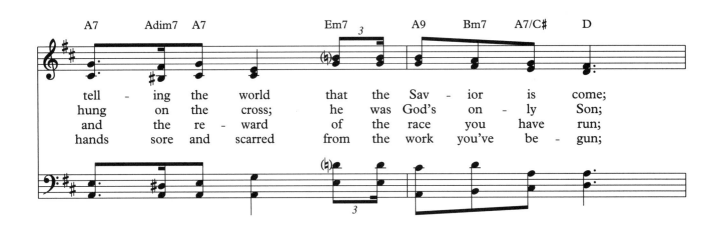

tell - ing the world that the Sav - ior is come;
hung on the cross; he was God's on - ly Son;
and the re - ward of the race you have run;
hands sore and scarred from the work you've be - gun;

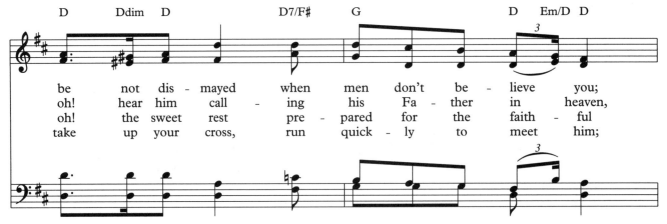

be not dis - mayed when men don't be - lieve you;
oh! hear him call - ing his Fa - ther in heaven,
oh! the sweet rest pre - pared for the faith - ful
take up your cross, run quick - ly to meet him;

This selection is often performed as a solo.

WORDS: Lucie E. Campbell
MUSIC: Lucie E. Campbell, arr. by Evelyn Simpson-Curenton

WELL DONE
10 10 10 8 with Refrain

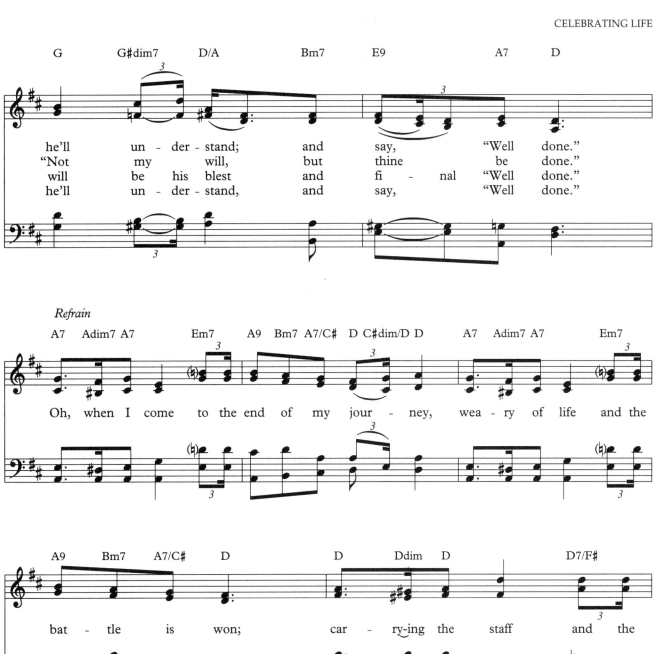

he'll un - der - stand; and say, "Well done."
"Not my will, but thine be done."
will be his blest and fi - nal "Well done."
he'll un - der - stand, and say, "Well done."

Refrain

Oh, when I come to the end of my jour - ney, wea - ry of life and the

bat - tle is won; car - ry-ing the staff and the

cross of re - demp - tion, he'll un - der-stand and say, "Well done."

139

Some Day

Yes, we do have confidence, and we would rather be away from the body
and at home with the Lord. (2 Corinthians 5:8)

Very slowly, with liberty (♩ = 60)

1. Beams of heav - en, as I go, through this wil - der - ness be -
2. Of - ten - times my sky is clear, joy a - bounds with - out a
3. Hard - er yet may be the fight, right may of - ten yield to
4. Bur - dens now may crush me down, dis - ap - point - ments all a -

low, · guide my feet in peace - ful ways, turn my mid - nights in - to
tear, though a day so bright be - gun, clouds may hide to - mor - row's
might, wick - ed - ness a - while may reign, Sa - tan's cause may seem to
round, trou - bles speak in mourn - ful sigh, sor - row through a tear - stained

days; when in the dark - ness I would grope, faith al - ways
sun. There'll be a day that's al - ways bright, a day that
gain; there is a God that rules a - bove, with hand of
eye; there is a world where plea - sure reigns, no mourn - ing

sees a star of hope, and soon from all life's grief and
nev - er yields to night, and in its light the streets of
pow'r and heart of love, if I am right, he'll fight my
soul shall roam its plains, and to that land of peace and

WORDS: Charles A. Tindley
MUSIC: Charles A. Tindley, arr. by F. A. Clark

SOMEDAY
77.77.88.96 with Refrain

dan - ger,   I shall be free   some day.
glo - ry   I shall be - hold   some day.
bat - tle,   I shall have peace   some day.   I do not
glo - ry   I want to go   some day.

know how long 'twill be,   nor what the fu - ture holds for me,   but this I

know,   if Je - sus leads me,   I shall get home   some day.

140

If I Can Help Somebody

*Therefore, my beloved, be steadfast, immovable, always excelling in the work of the Lord,
because you know that in the Lord your labor is not in vain. (1 Corinthians 15:58)*

This selection is usually performed as a solo.

WORDS: A. Bazel Androzzo
MUSIC: A. Bazel Androzzo, arr. by Kenneth Morris

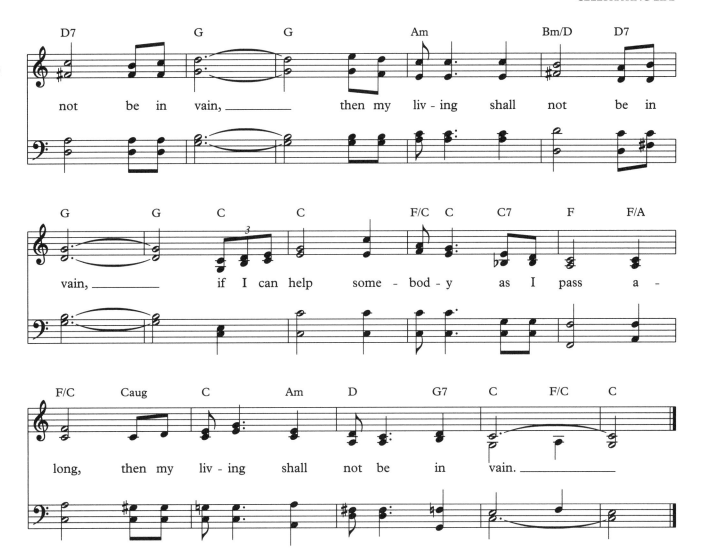

141 Guide My Feet

Guide our feet into the way of peace. (Luke 1:79b)

WORDS: African American spiritual
MUSIC: African American spiritual, harm. by Dr. Wendell P. Whalum

Come, Come! Ev'rybody Come!

"If you have judged me to be faithful to the Lord, come and stay at my home." (Acts 16:15b)

See Performance Notes.

WORDS: Marilyn E. Thornton
MUSIC: Marilyn E. Thornton

© 2001 Marilyn E. Thornton

Welcome into This Place

Lift up your heads, O gates! and be lifted up, O ancient doors!
that the King of glory may come in. (Psalm 24:9)

WORDS: Orlando Juarez
MUSIC: Orlando Juarez, arr. by Jimmie Abbington and Darryl Glenn Nettles

Lord, You Are Welcome

So he hurried down and was happy to welcome him. (Luke 19:6)

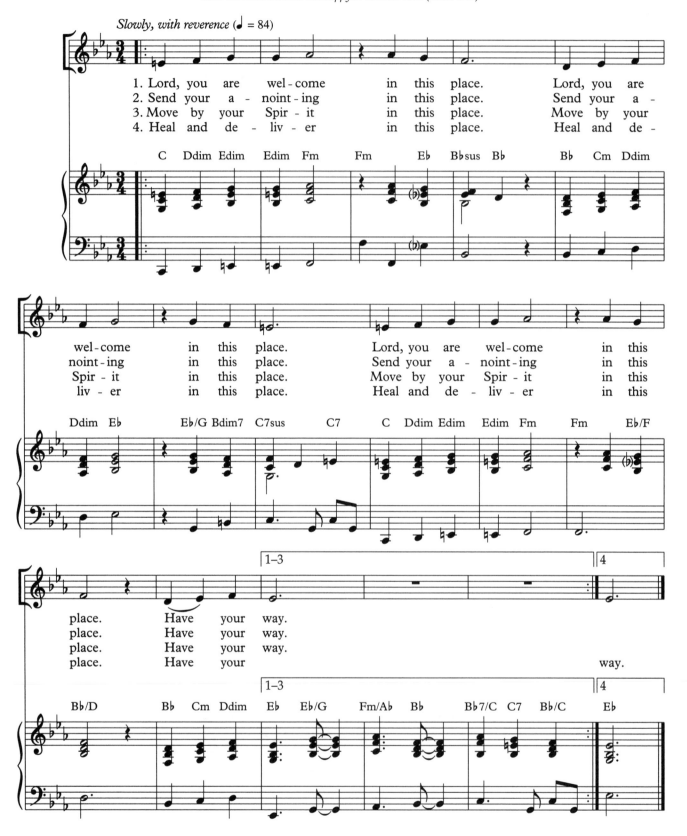

WORDS: Kurt Lykes
MUSIC: Kurt Lykes, arr. by Cynthia Wilson

Here I Am to Worship

O come, let us worship and bow down, let us kneel before the LORD, our Maker! (Psalm 95:6)

1. Light of the world, you stepped down into darkness,
2. King of all days, oh, so highly exalted,

o-pen my eyes let me ___ see beau-ty that made this
glo-rious in heav-en a – bove. Hum – bly you came to the

heart a – dore you, hope of a life spent with __ you.
earth you cre-at – ed, all for love's sake be-came __ poor.

So here I am to

WORDS: Tim Hughes
MUSIC: Tim Hughes, arr. by Cynthia Wilson

Just One Word from You

One does not live by bread alone,
but by every word that comes from the mouth of the LORD. (Deuteronomy 8:3b)

WORDS: Eli Wilson, Jr.
MUSIC: Eli Wilson, Jr.
© 1995 Eli Wilson, Jr.

God Is Here

*"Come to me, all you that are weary and are carrying heavy burdens,
and I will give you rest." (Matthew 11:28)*

WORDS: Martha Munizzi, Israel Houghton, and Meleasa Houghton
MUSIC: Martha Munizzi, Israel Houghton, and Meleasa Houghton, arr. by Cynthia Wilson

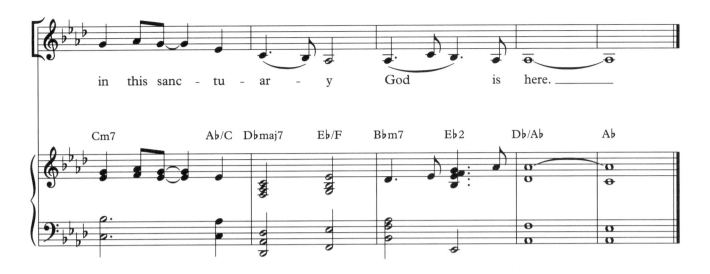

in this sanc - tu - ar - y   God   is here. _____

Jesu Tawa Pano/Jesus, We Are Here

148

When the day of Pentecost had come, they were all together in one place. (Acts 2:1)

Je - su ta - wa pa - no; Je - su ta - wa pa - no;
Je - sus, we are here; Je - sus, we are here;

Solo *Ma-mbo Je - su.

Je - su ta - wa pa - no; ta - wa pa - no, mu zi - ta re - nyu.
Je - sus, we are here; we are here for you.

Omit last time.

Shona Transliteration:
Yah-zoo tah-wah pah-no
tah-wah pah-no, moo zee-tah ray-noo (mahm-bo Yah-zoo)

WORDS: Patrick Matsikenyiri (Zimbabwe)
MUSIC: Patrick Matsikenyiri

MATSIKENYIRI
Irregular

149

Standin' in the Need of Prayer

Give praise, O servants of the LORD, you that stand in the house of the LORD,
in the courts of the house of our God. (Psalm 135:1b, 2)

1. Not my broth-er, nor my sis-ter, but it's me, O Lord,
2. Not the preach-er, nor the dea-con, but it's me, O Lord,
3. Not my fa-ther, nor my moth-er, but it's me, O Lord,
4. Not the stran-ger, nor my neigh-bor, but it's me, O Lord,

stand-in' in the need of prayer; not my broth-er, nor my sis-ter, but it's
stand-in' in the need of prayer; not the preach-er, nor the dea-con, but it's
stand-in' in the need of prayer; not my fa-ther, nor my moth-er, but it's
stand-in' in the need of prayer; not the stran-ger, nor my neigh-bor, but it's

me, O Lord, stand-in' in the need of prayer.
me, O Lord, stand-in' in the need of prayer.
me, O Lord, stand-in' in the need of prayer.
me, O Lord, stand-in' in the need of prayer.

It's me, it's me, O Lord,

stand-in' in the need of prayer; it's me, it's me, O Lord, stand-in' in the need of prayer.

WORDS: African American spiritual
MUSIC: African American spiritual

Arr. © 1981 Abingdon Press

Early in the Morning

150

O God, you are my God, I seek you, my soul thirsts for you. (Psalm 63:1a)

Slowly, with movement (♩ = 68)

Ear-ly in the morn-ing _____ I will seek your face.

Long-ing for your fav - or, _____ thirst-ing for your grace, clear-ing all the

clut - ter _____ be-fore the day be-gins, I in-vite you

in, my God, my King. _____ Ear-ly in the King. _____

To repeat | *Song ending*

WORDS: Johnetta Johnson Page
MUSIC: Johnetta Johnson Page

151

Living in the Imagination of God

"What no eye has seen, nor ear heard, nor the human heart conceived,
what God has prepared for those who love him." (1 Corinthians 2:9)

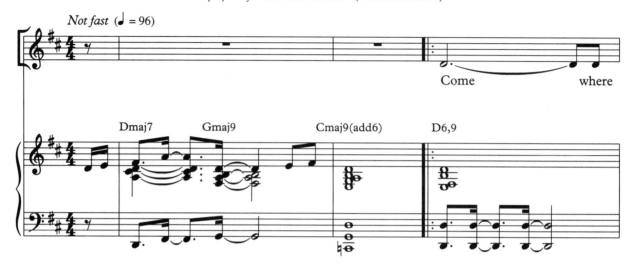

Come where

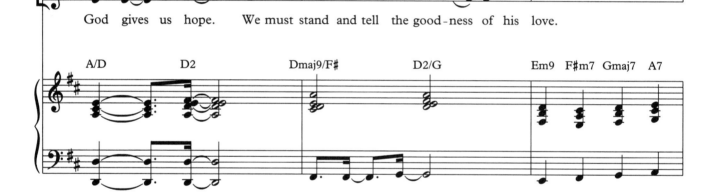

God gives us hope. We must stand and tell the good-ness of his love.

Share in God's dream, where we show grace to all peo - ple. We are

WORDS: Cecilia Olusola Tribble
MUSIC: Cecilia Olusola Tribble
© 2007 Cecilia Olusola Tribble

369

152

Walking Up the King's Highway

I will make them strong in the LORD, and they shall walk in his name. (Zechariah 10:12)

1. My way gets bright-er, my load gets light-er,
2. Don't have to wor-ry, don't have to hur-ry, walk-ing up the King's high-
3. If you're not walk-ing, start while I'm talk-ing,

way,
there's joy in know-ing with God I'm go-ing,
Christ walks be-side me an - gels to guide me,
there'll be a bless-ing you'll be pos-sess-ing,

WORDS: Mary Gardner and Thomas Dorsey
MUSIC: Mary Gardner and Thomas Dorsey, arr. by Monya Davis Logan

KING'S HIGHWAY
55 7 55 7 with Refrain

Holy Is His Name

Having become as much superior to angels
as the name he has inherited is more excellent than theirs. (Hebrews 1:4)

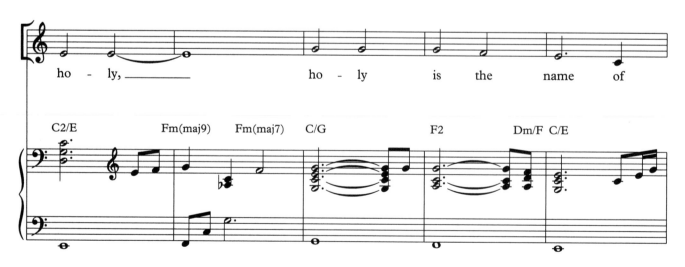

WORDS: Leon Lewis
MUSIC: Leon Lewis

© 2002 Meadowgreen Music Company (ASCAP), admin. by EMI CMG Publishing

154 Hold to God's Unchanging Hand

For I, the LORD your God, hold your right hand;
it is I who say to you, "Do not fear, I will help you." (Isaiah 41:13)

WORDS: Jennie Wilson
MUSIC: F. L. Eiland, arr. by Stephen Key
Arr. © 2000 GIA Publications, Inc.

UNCHANGING HAND
87 87 with Refrain

Hold to his hand, _ God's un - chang - ing hand. _

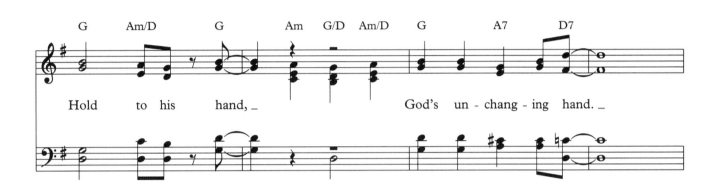

Hold to his hand, _ God's un - chang - ing hand. _

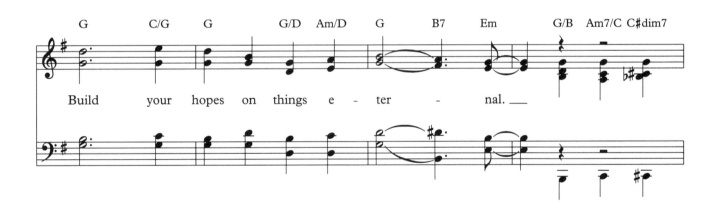

Build your hopes on things e - ter - nal. __

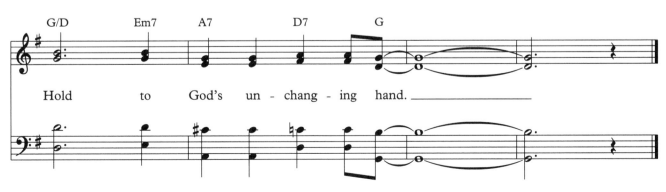

Hold to God's un - chang - ing hand. _____

155

Heavenly Father

For if you forgive others their trespasses,
your heavenly Father will also forgive you. (Matthew 6:14)

See Performance Notes.

WORDS: Frederick Burchell
MUSIC: Frederick Burchell, transcribed by William S. Moon

© 2007 B4 Entertainment

384

385

390

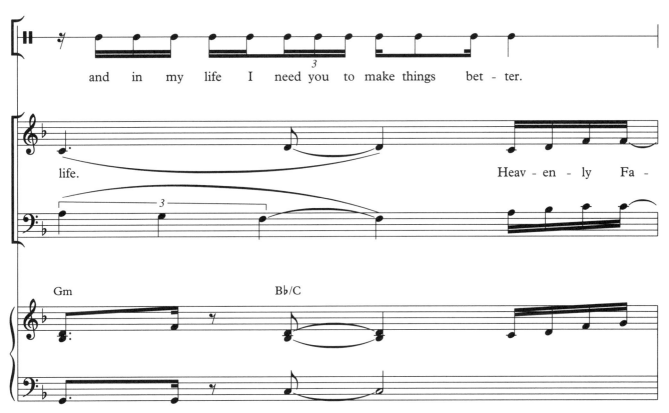

393

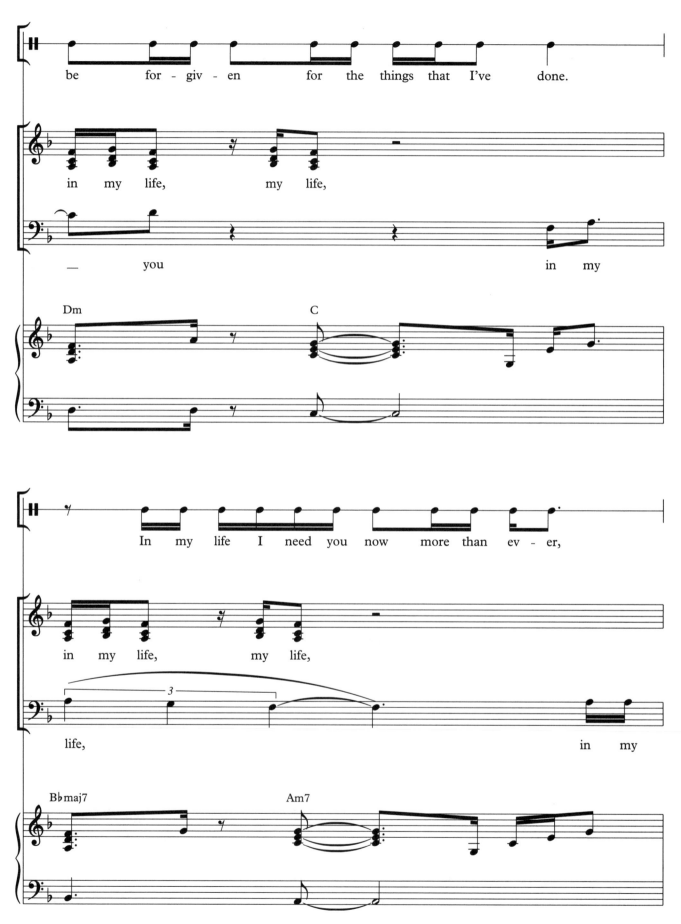

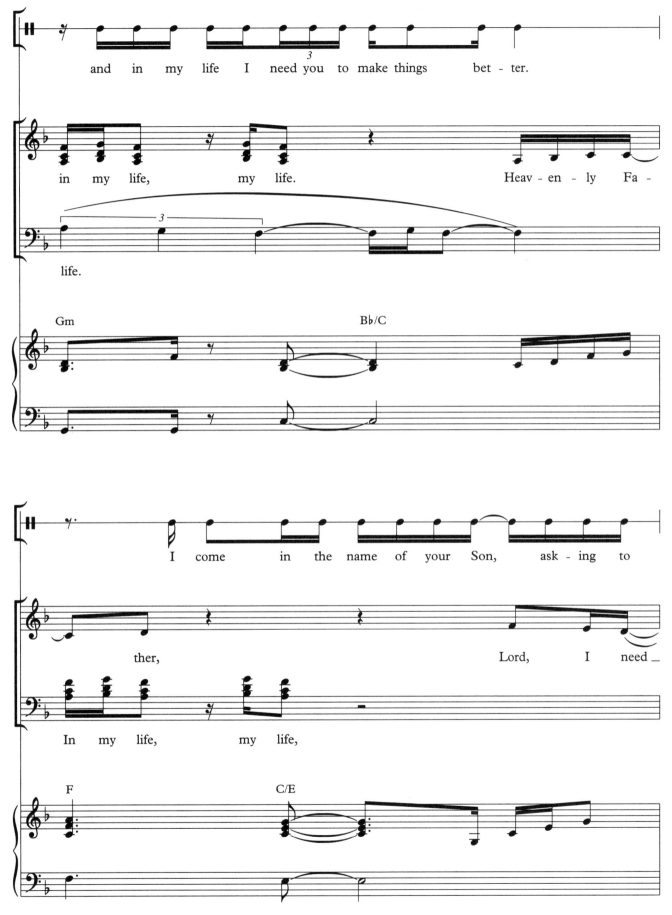

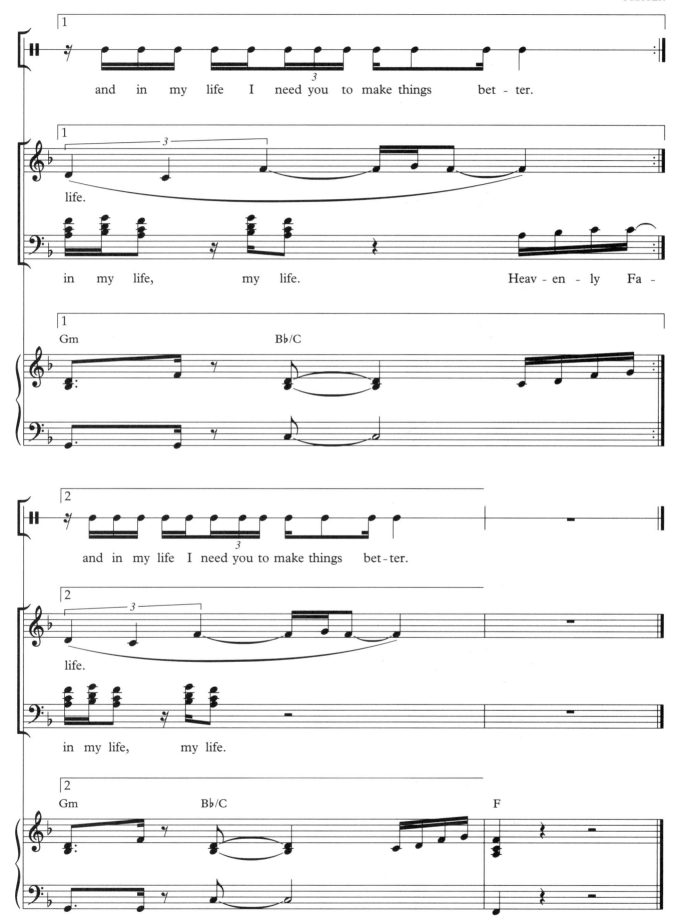

Heavenly Father

Bass

MUSIC: Frederick Burchell, transcribed by William S. Moon

© 2007 B4 Entertainment

Heavenly Father

Drums

MUSIC: Frederick Burchell, transcribed by William S. Moon

405

156
Lord, Listen to Your Children Praying

"From the lips of children and infants you have ordained praise." (Matthew 21:16b NIV)

Lord, lis-ten to your chil-dren pray-ing, _____ Lord, send your Spir-it in this place; _____ Lord, lis-ten to your chil-dren pray-ing, _____ send us love, send us power, send us grace. _____

WORDS: Ken Medema
MUSIC: Ken Medema
© 1973 Hope Publishing Co.

CHILDREN PRAYING
98.99

157
Precious Jesus

For I am not ashamed of the gospel; it is the power of God for salvation to everyone who has faith, to the Jew first and also to the Greek. (Romans 1:16)

Pre-cious Je-sus, how I love you, how I lift high my voice with your praise. Ho-ly

May be played one octave lower.

WORDS: Thomas A. Whitfield
MUSIC: Thomas A. Whitfield, arr. by William S. Moon

Arr. © 2007 Abingdon Press, admin. by The Copyright Co.

Spir-it, I im-plore thee, drench my heart as my lips 'part your grace. Pre-cious grace.

I am per-suad-ed, Lord, to love you. I have been changed to bless your name.

wor - ship
I am con-strained by the great gos-pel, for-ev-er to wor-ship thee.

407

158

Remember Me

Remember not the sins of my youth, nor my transgressions;
according to thy mercy remember thou me for thy goodness' sake, O LORD. (Psalm 25:7 KJV)

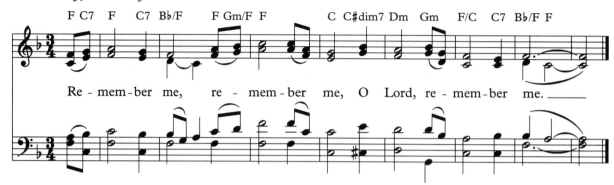

Re - mem - ber me, re - mem - ber me, O Lord, re - mem - ber me. _____

WORDS: Trad.
MUSIC: Trad., harm. by J. Jefferson Cleveland
Harm. © 1981 Abingdon Press, admin. by The Copyright Co.

159

Thy Way, O Lord

Thy kingdom come. Thy will be done in earth, as it is in heaven. (Matthew 6:10 KJV)

1. Thy way, O Lord, not mine, thy will be done not mine; since
2. Thy way, O Lord, not mine, let glo - ry all be thine; keep
3. Hide me from self, O Lord, may I at - tend thy word; send
4. Sub - mis - sive - ly, I bow; with strength and grace en - dow this

WORDS: Nina B. Jackson
MUSIC: E. C. Deas, arr. by Darryl Glenn Nettles
Arr. © 2007 Abingdon Press, admin. by The Copyright Co.

THY WAY
66 666 4 with Refrain

You Are the One

O Lord, all my longing is known to you;
my sighing is not hidden from you. (Psalm 38:9)

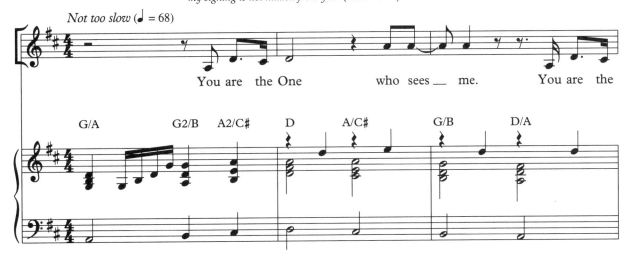

You are the One who sees __ me. You are the

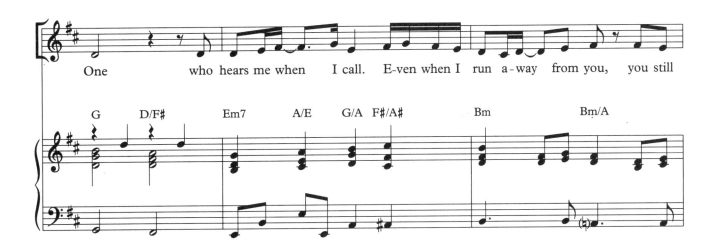

One who hears me when I call. E-ven when I run a-way from you, you still

speak my name call-ing me back to you. __ You are the

WORDS: Jonathan Cole Dow and Johnetta Johnson Page
MUSIC: Jonathan Cole Dow and Johnetta Johnson Page, arr. by William S. Moon
© 2002 Jonathan Cole Dow

161

He's Sweet, I Know

How sweet are your words to my taste, sweeter than honey to my mouth! (Psalm 119:103)

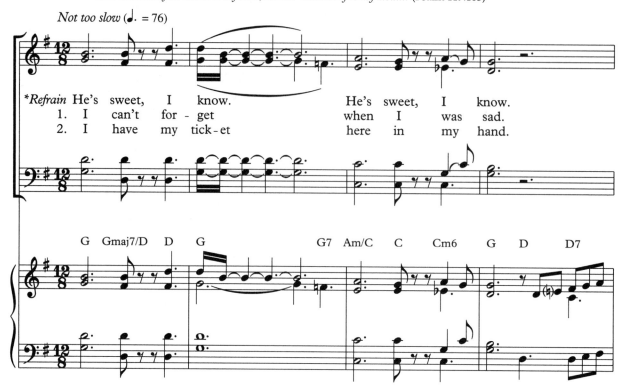

*Refrain He's sweet, I know. He's sweet, I know.
1. I can't for-get when I was sad.
2. I have my tick-et here in my hand.

G Gmaj7/D D G G7 Am/C C Cm6 G D D7

Storm clouds may rise, strong winds may blow.
Head hang-ing down, soul feel-ing bad.
I'm go-ing to that beau-ti-ful land.

G Em D G B Em A9 F#m/A A7 D7 G/D C#dim7 D7/F#

*Refrain may be sung after each stanza.

WORDS: Trad. Gospel hymn
MUSIC: Trad. Gospel hymn, arr. by Kenneth Lewis and Nolan Williams, Jr.

HE'S SWEET
88 9 11

I'll tell the world wher - ev - er I go. That
All I could say was Lord take my heart. —
Some - time I weep and some - time I moan. But

G Gmaj7/D D G G7 Am/C C Cm6 G Am Bb B7 D#dim7

I've found a Sav - ior, and he's sweet, I know.
Je - sus heard and saved me, and gave me a start.
I'm bound for glo - ry, and I'm go - ing on.

Em Cm/Eb Cm6 G Fmaj7 E7(b9) Am G/B Am/C G/D D7 G

You Are Holy

Holy, holy, holy, the Lord God the Almighty, who was and is and is to come. (Revelation 4:8c)

WORDS: Cecilia L. Clemons
MUSIC: Cecilia L. Clemons

*To optional modulations for verses 3 and 4.

417

163

Just a Little Talk with Jesus

It is Christ Jesus, who died, yes, who was raised,
who is at the right hand of God, who indeed intercedes for us. (Romans 8:34b)

1. I once was lost in sin but Jesus took me in, and
2. Some-times my path seems drear, with-out a ray of cheer, and
3. I may have doubts and fears, my eyes be filled with tears, but

then a lit-tle light from heav-en filled my soul; it
then a cloud of doubt may hide the light of day; the
Je-sus is a friend who watch-es day and night; I

bathed my heart in love and wrote my name a-bove, and
mists of sin may rise and hide the star-ry skies, but
go to him in prayer, he knows my ev-ery care, and

just a lit-tle talk with Je-sus made me whole.
just a lit-tle talk with Je-sus clears the way.
just a lit-tle talk with Je-sus makes it right.

Refrain

Now let us

WORDS: Cleavant Derricks
MUSIC: Ceavant Derricks

© 1937 Stamps-Baxter Music (BMI), admin. by Brentwood-Benson Music Publishing, Inc.

JUST A LITTLE TALK
66 12 66 12 with refrain

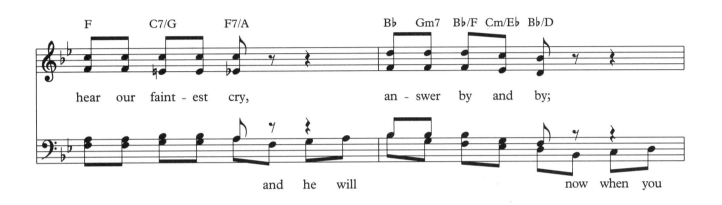

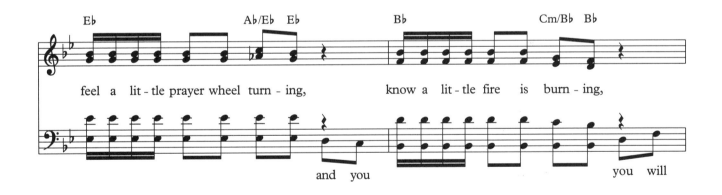

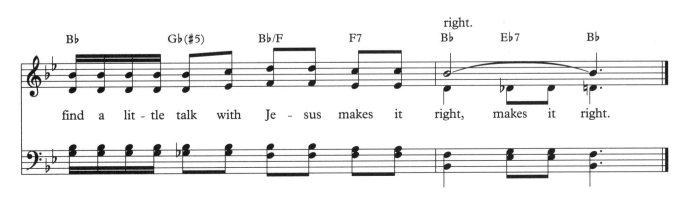

Stand by Me

But God's firm foundation stands, bearing this inscription:
"The Lord knows those who are his." (2 Timothy 2:19a)

Reverently, moderate speed

1. When the storms of life are rag-ing, when the
2. In the midst of trib-u-la-tion, in the
3. In the midst of faults and fail-ures, stand by me; in the
4. In the midst of per-se-cu-tion, in the
5. When I'm grow-ing old and fee-ble, When I'm

storms of life are rag-ing, When the
midst of trib-u-la-tion, When the
midst of faults and fail-ures, stand by me. When I
midst of per-se-cu-tion, When my
grow-ing old and fee-ble, When my

world is toss-ing me like a ship up-on the sea; thou who
hosts of hell as-sail, and my strength be-gins to fail, thou who
do the best I can, and my friends mis-un-der-stand, thou who
foes in bat-tle ar-ray un-der-take to stop my way, thou who
life be-comes a bur-den and I'm near-ing chil-ly Jor-dan, O thou

WORDS: Charles Albert Tindley
MUSIC: Charles Albert Tindley, arr. by J. Jefferson Cleveland and Verolga Nix

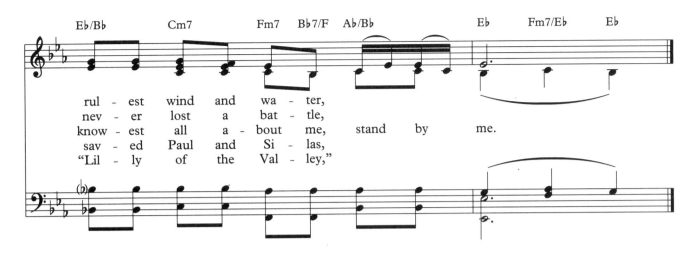

rul - est wind and wa - ter,
nev - er lost a bat - tle,
know - est all a - bout me, stand by me.
sav - ed Paul and Si - las,
"Lil - ly of the Val - ley,"

Sanctuary

*May the God of peace himself sanctify you entirely; and may your spirit and soul and body
be kept sound and blameless at the coming of our Lord Jesus Christ.* (1 Thessalonians 5:23)

165

Lord, pre - pare me to be a sanc - tu - ar - y, pure and

ho - ly, tried and true; with thanks - giv - ing, I'll be a

liv - ing sanc - tu - ar - y for you.

WORDS: John Thompson and Randy Scruggs
MUSIC: John Thompson and Randy Scruggs

SANCTUARY
Irregular

Somebody Prayed for Me

Pray for one another, so that you may be healed. (James 5:16*b*)

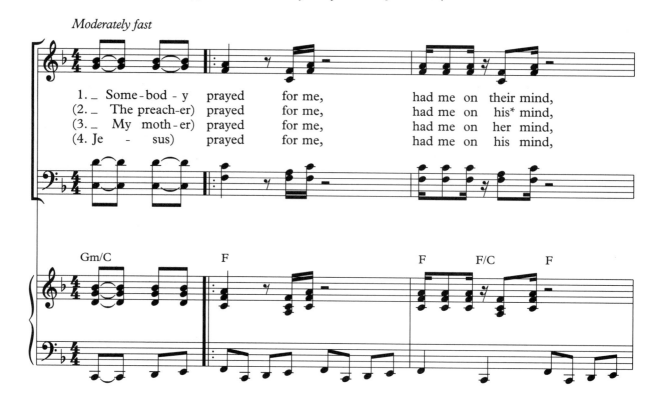

Use "her" on verse two as appropriate.

WORDS: Dorothy Norwood and Alvin Darling
MUSIC: Dorothy Norwood and Alvin Darling, arr. by Nolan Williams, Jr. and Stephen Key
© 1994 Malaco Music Co. (BMI)

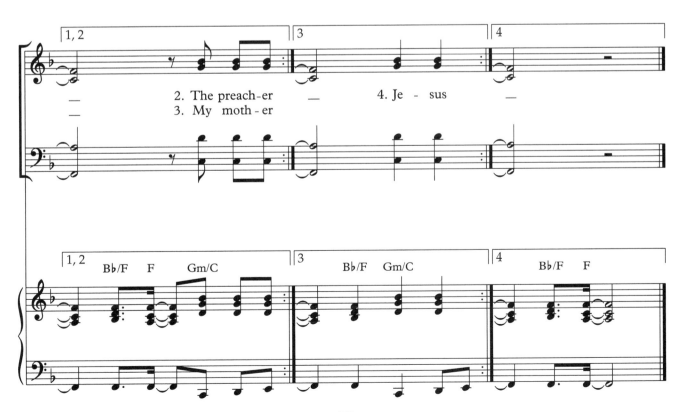

167

Learning to Lean

Trust in the LORD with all thine heart;
and lean not unto thine own understanding. (Proverbs 3:5 KJV)

Learn-ing to lean, learn-ing to lean, I'm learn-ing to lean on Je - sus.

Find-ing more pow-er than I've ev-er seen. I'm learn-ing to lean on Je - sus.

WORDS: John Stallings
MUSIC: John Stallings, arr. by Evelyn Simpson-Curenton

168

We'll Understand It Better By and By

Now I know only in part; then I will know fully,
even as I have been fully known. (1 Corinthians 13:12b)

1. We are tossed and driv - en on this rest-less sea of time som - ber
2. We are of-ten des-ti-tute of the things that life de-mands want of
3. Tri - als dark on ev-ery hand and we can-not un-der-stand all the
4. Temp - ta-tions hid-den snares of-ten take us un-a-wares, and our

WORDS: Charles Albert Tindley
MUSIC: Charles Albert Tindley, arr. by Theodore Thomas

BY AND BY
77 15 77 11 with Refrain

We Offer Christ

For we do not proclaim ourselves; we proclaim Jesus Christ as Lord
and ourselves as your slaves for Jesus' sake. (2 Corinthians 4:5)

We of-fer Christ to you, oh, my

broth-er, we of-fer Christ to you, oh, my sis-ter. He will

WORDS: Joel Britton
MUSIC: Joel Britton, arr. by Valeria A. Foster

428

170

Praise You

And it is no longer I who live, but it is Christ who lives in me. And the life I now live in the flesh
I live by faith in the Son of God, who loved me and gave himself for me. (Galatians 2:20)

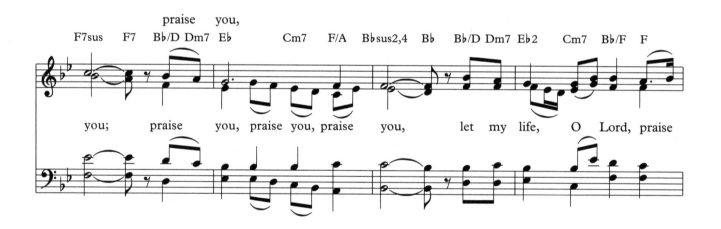

WORDS: Elizabeth Goodine
MUSIC: Elizabeth Goodine

Come unto Jesus

"Come to me, all you that are weary and are carrying heavy burdens,
and I will give you rest." (Matthew 11:28)

WORDS: Raymond Wise
MUSIC: Raymond Wise

© 1991 Raise Publishing Company

172 Yes, God Is Real

For I know that my Redeemer lives, and that at the last he will stand upon the earth. (Job 19:25)

With movement (no faster than ♩. = 63)

1. There are some things   I may not know,   there are some
2. Some folks may doubt,   some folks may scorn,   all can de -
3. I can-not tell   just how you felt   when Je - sus

Cm7/F   Bbmaj7   Gm7 F#m7 Fm7 Bb9sus   Ebmaj7   Edim7

plac - es I can-not go,   but I am sure   of this one
sert and leave me a-lone,   but as for me   I'll take God's
took your sins a - way,   but since that day,   yes, since that

Bb/F   Cm7/F   Bb   Cm7/F   Bbmaj7   Gm7 F#m7 Fm7 Bb9sus

thing,   that God is real   for I can feel   him deep with -
part,   for God is real   and I can feel   him in my
hour,   God has been real   for I can feel   his ho - ly

Ebmaj7   Edim7   Bb/F   Gm7   Cm11   F7

WORDS: Kenneth Morris
MUSIC: Kenneth Morris, arr. by Oscar Dismuke

GOD IS REAL
8 9 8 12 with Refrain

173
Lead Me, Guide Me

Teach me thy way, O LORD, and lead me in a plain path. (Psalm 27:11 KJV)

Lead me, guide me, a - long the way,

for if you lead me, I can - not stray. Lord, let me

walk each day with thee. Lead me, O Lord, lead me. _____

Fine

WORDS: Doris Akers
MUSIC: Doris Akers

LEAD ME, GUIDE ME
Irregular with Refrain

Center of My Joy

And not only so, but we also joy in God through our Lord Jesus Christ,
by whom we have now received the atonement. (Romans 5:11 KJV)

Je - sus, you're the cen - ter of my joy, _____

all that's good and per - fect comes from you. _____

WORDS: Richard Smallwood, William Gaither, Gloria Gaither
MUSIC: Richard Smallwood, William Gaither, Gloria Gaither, arr. by Mark A. Miller

CENTER OF MY JOY
Irregular

I'm Determined

Beloved, I do not consider that I have made it my own, but this one thing I do: forgetting
what lies behind and straining forward to what lies ahead, I press on. (Philippians 3:13-14a)

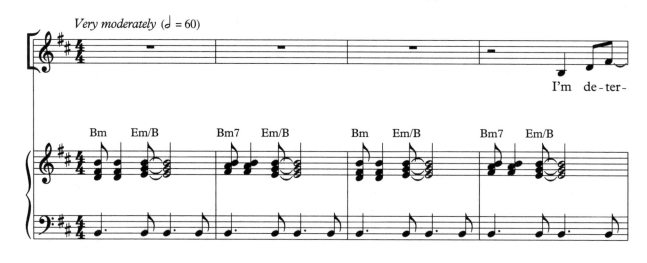

Each section can be repeated as desired.

WORDS: African American trad.
MUSIC: African American trad., arr. by Marilyn E. Thornton

All sections may be repeated as desired.

I Love the Lord

I love the LORD, because he has heard my voice and my supplications. (Psalm 116:1)

WORDS: Richard Smallwood
MUSIC: Richard Smallwood, arr. by Nolan Williams, Jr.

I Will Bow to You

"But if not, be it known to you, O king, that we will not serve your gods
and we will not worship the golden statue that you have set up." (Daniel 3:18)

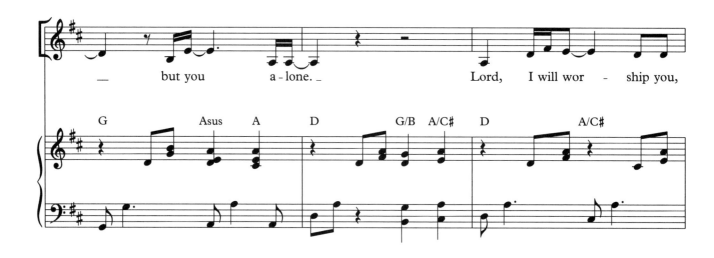

WORDS: Pete Episcopo
MUSIC: Pete Episcopo, arr. by Mark A. Miller
© 2001 Integrity's Hosanna Music

down my i - dols, thrones I have made,

Em7   D/F♯

all that has tak - en my heart. _ Lord, I will bow to you,

G   D/F♯   Asus A G/B A/C♯ D   A/C♯

to no oth - er God _ but you a - lone. _

Bm7   D/F♯   G   Asus A   D

178 Change My Heart, O God

Yet, O LORD, you are our Father; we are the clay, and you are our potter;
we are all the work of your hand. (Isaiah 64:8)

Slowly, with reverence

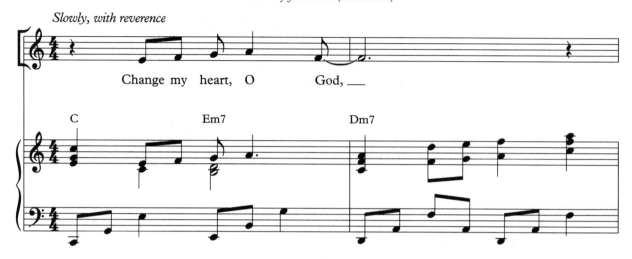

WORDS: Eddie Espinosa
MUSIC: Eddie Espinosa

© 1982 Mercy/Vineyard Publishing, admin. by Music Services

CHANGE MY HEART
Irregular

God Has Done Great Things for Me

179

The LORD has done great things for us, and we rejoiced. (Psalm 126:3)

*May substitute "God."

WORDS: Jessy Dixon
MUSIC: Jessy Dixon, arr. by Stephen Key

GREAT THINGS
7.4.7

Completely Yes

And she answered and said unto him, "Yes, Lord." (Mark 7:28a KJV)

WORDS: Sandra Crouch
MUSIC: Sandra Crouch, arr. by Stephen Key

He's My Foundation

181

Very moderately (♩ = 96)

Built upon the foundation of the apostles and prophets, with Christ Jesus himself as the cornerstone. (Ephesians 2:20)

Refrain

Leader

No mat-ter what you're fac-ing   When storms keep on rag-ing   Giv-er

People

He's my foun-da-tion.   He's my foun-da-tion.

of Sal-va-tion   That's why I got-ta praise him   *Verse* 1. When

He's my foun-da-tion.   He's my foun-da-tion.

trials and tests   try to get me at my best   I still

He's my foun-da-tion.   He's my foun-da-tion.

know I'm blessed   I've built my life on Christ.   2. When this

He's my foun-da-tion.   I've built my life on Christ.

See Performance Notes.
WORDS: Frederick Burchell
MUSIC: Frederick Burchell, transcribed by William S. Moon
© 2007 B4 Entertainment

The Solid Rock

But it did not fall, because it had been founded on rock. (Matthew 7:25b)

See Performance Note for no. 181.

WORDS: Edward Mote
MUSIC: William B. Bradbury, arr. by Johnetta Page and Jonathan Dow

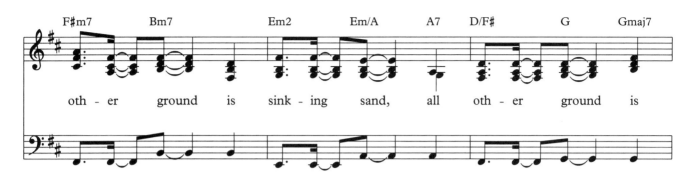

oth - er ground is sink - ing sand, all oth - er ground is

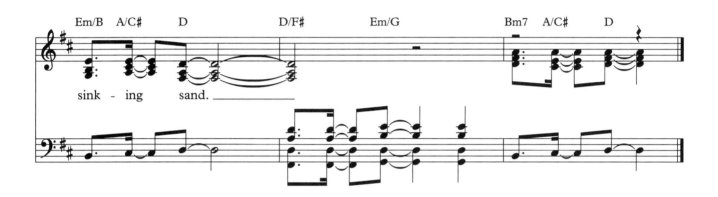

sink - ing sand. _____

183

Yes, Lord, Yes

"I delight to do your will, O my God; your law is within my heart." (Psalm 40:8)

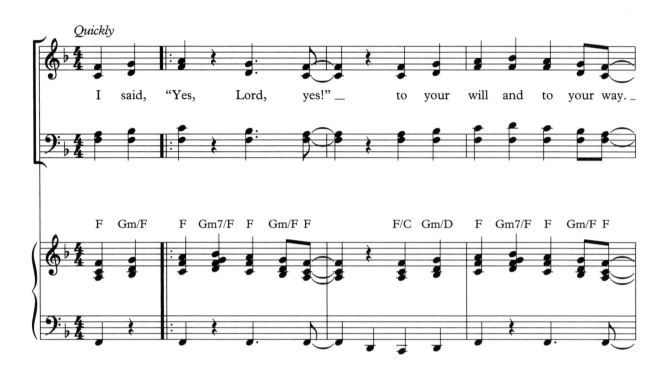

WORDS: Lynn Keesecker
MUSIC: Lynn Keesecker, arr. by Marilyn E. Thornton
© 1983 Manna Music, Inc.

You Are My All in All

"I am the Alpha and Omega," says the Lord God,
who is and who was and who is to come, the Almighty. (Revelation 1:8)

WORDS: Dennis Jernigan
MUSIC: Dennis Jernigan, arr. by William S. Moon

fool. You are my all in all.
cup. You are my all in all.

1. You are my strength when I am weak. You are the treas-ure that I
2. Tak-ing my sin, my cross, my shame, ris-ing a-gain I bless your

Je - sus, Lamb of God,

Never Been Scared

185

So then, brothers and sisters, stand firm and hold fast to the traditions that you were taught by us. (2 Thessalonians 2:15a)

See Performance Notes.

WORDS: Frederick Burchell
MUSIC: Frederick Burchell, transcribed by William Moon

© 2007 B4 Entertainment

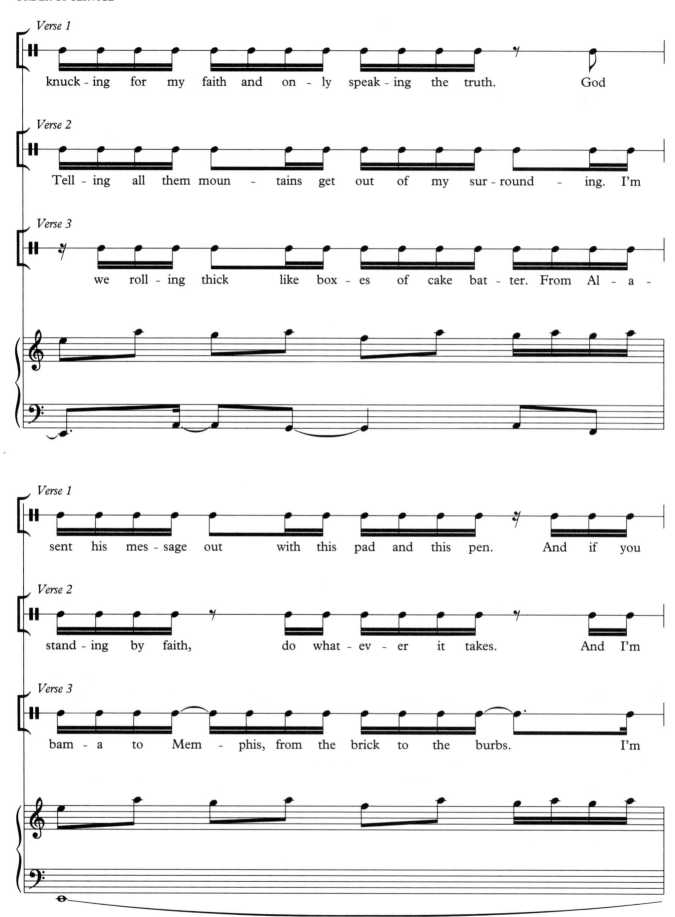

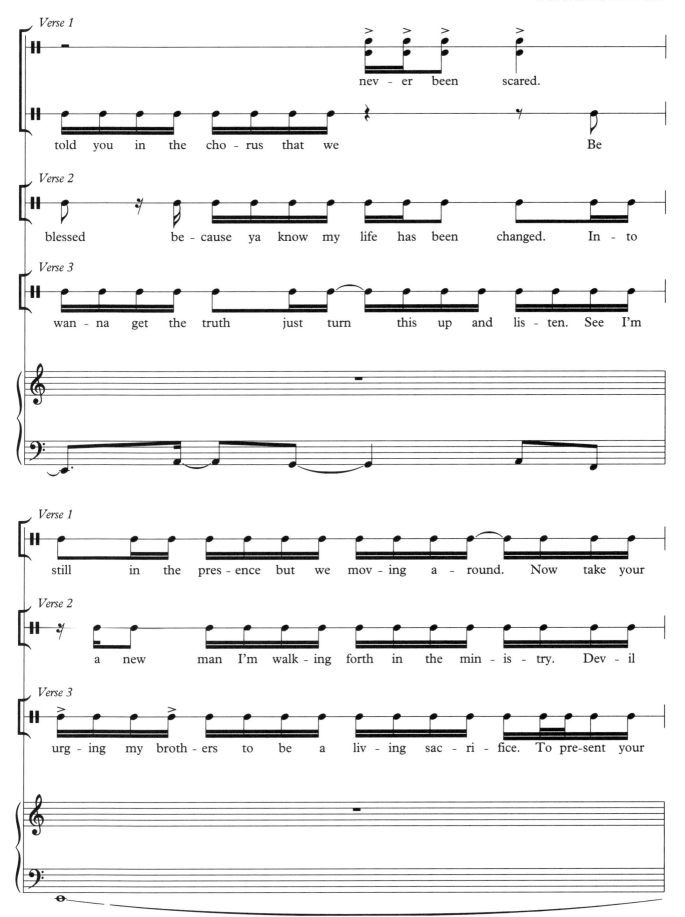

185

Never Been Scared

Synthesizer 1

MUSIC: Frederick Burchell, transcribed by William Moon

© 2007 B4 Entertainment

Never Been Scared

MUSIC: Frederick Burchell, transcribed by William Moon

© 2007 B4 Entertainment

185

Never Been Scared

Piano

MUSIC: Frederick Burchell, transcribed by William Moon

Never Been Scared

Drum Set

Not fast (♩ = 80)

MUSIC: Frederick Burchell, transcribed by William Moon

I Will Arise

"I will get up and go to my father." (Luke 15:18a)

1. Come, ye sin-ners, poor and need-y, weak and wound-ed, sick and sore;
2. Come, ye thirst-y, come, and wel-come, God's free boun-ty glo-ri-fy;
3. Come, ye wea-ry, heav-y-lad-en, lost and ru-ined by the fall;

Je-sus read-y stands to save you, full of pit-y, love, and power.
true be-lief and true re-pen-tance, ev-ery grace that brings you nigh.
if you tar-ry till you're bet-ter, you will nev-er come at all.

I will a-rise and go to Je-sus, he will em-brace me in his arms;

in the arms of my dear Sav-ior, O there are ten thou-sand charms.

WORDS: Joseph Hart
MUSIC: Walker's *Southern Harmony*, 1835

RESTORATION
8 7 8 7 with Refrain

My Soul Loves Jesus

I love you, O LORD, my strength. (Psalm 18:1)

1. My soul loves Je-sus, my soul loves Je-sus, my soul loves Je-sus; bless his name.
2. He's a won-der in my soul, he's a won-der in my soul, he's a won-der in my soul; bless his name.
3. My soul seeks to please him, my soul seeks to please him, my soul seeks to please him; bless his name.

1. My soul loves Je-sus, my soul loves Je-sus, my soul loves Je-sus; bless his name.
2. He's a won-der in my soul, he's a won-der in my soul, he's a won-der in my soul; bless his name.
3. My soul seeks to please him, my soul seeks to please him, my soul seeks to please him; bless his name.

WORDS: Charles H. Mason
MUSIC: Charles H. Mason, arr. by Iris Stevenson
© 1982 The Church of God in Christ Publishing Board

MY SOUL LOVES JESUS
Irregular

ORDER OF SERVICE

188

Come, Be Baptized

And people kept coming and were being baptized. (John 3:23b)

WORDS: Gary Alan Smith
MUSIC: Gary Alan Smith
© 1982 Hope Publishing Co.

COME, BE BAPTIZED
Irregular with Refrain

wash in the love that is sent from a - bove.
feel how it pours out the life that is yours.

Refrain

Come, be bap-tized in the name of the Fa - ther.

Come, be bap-tized in the name of the Son.

Wade in the Water

189

Moses stretched out his hand over the sea. The LORD drove the sea back
by a strong east wind all night, and turned the sea into dry land. (Exodus 14:21)

WORDS: African American spiritual
MUSIC: African American spiritual, arr. by Monya Davis Logan

WADE IN THE WATER
Irregular with Refrain

190

Take Me to the Water

"Look, here is water! What is to prevent me from being baptized?" (Acts 8:37)

WORDS: African American traditional
MUSIC: African American traditional, arr. by Marilyn E. Thornton
Arr. © 2007 Abingdon Press, admin. by The Copyright Co.

TO THE WATER
Irregular

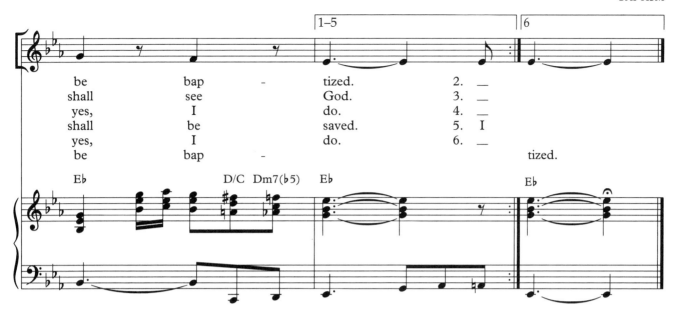

191 Wash, O God, Our Sons and Daughters

But when they believed Philip, who was proclaiming the good news about the kingdom of God and the name of Jesus Christ, they were baptized, both men and women. (Acts 8:12)

1. Wash, O God, our sons and daugh-ters, where your cleans-ing wa-ters flow. Num-ber them a-mong your peo-ple; bless as Christ blessed long a-go. Weave them gar-ments bright and spar-kling; Com-pass them with love and light. Fill, a-noint them; send your Spir-it, Ho-ly dove and heart's de-light.

2. We who bring them long for nur-ture; by your milk may we be fed. Let us join your feast, par-tak-ing cup of bless-ing, liv-ing bread. God, re-new us, guide our foot-steps; free from sin and all its snares, one with Christ in liv-ing, dy-ing, by your Spir-it, chil-dren, heirs.

3. O how deep your ho-ly wis-dom! Un-i-mag-ined, all your ways! To your name be glo-ry, hon-or! With our lives we wor-ship, praise! We your peo-ple stand be-fore you, wa-ter-washed and Spir-it-born. By your grace, our lives we of-fer. Re-cre-ate us; God, trans-form!

WORDS: Ruth Duck
MUSIC: Attr. to B. F. White, harm. by Ronald A. Nelson

BEACH SPRING
8 7 8 7

I've Just Come from the Fountain

"To the thirsty I will give water as a gift from the spring of the water of life." (Revelation 21:6b)

Refrain

I've just come from the foun-tain, I've just come from the foun-tain, Lord, I've

just come from the foun-tain, his name's so sweet. O Lord, I've sweet. | Fine

Leader ... *All*

1. O broth-er, do you love Je-sus? Yes, yes, I do love my Je-sus.

Leader ... *All* ... *D.S.*

Broth-er, do you love Je-sus? His name's so sweet. O Lord, I've

2. O sister, do you love Jesus …
3. O sinner, do you love Jesus …

WORDS: African American spiritual
MUSIC: African American spiritual, arr. by James Capers

Arr. © 1995 Augsburg Fortress

HIS NAME SO SWEET
88.74 with Refrain

Water Flowing Free

Then the angel showed me the river of the water of life, bright as crystal,
flowing from the throne of God and of the Lamb. (Revelation 22:1)

1. Wa-ter flow - ing, flow - ing free, streams of
(2. Like the) flood up - on the earth claim-ing
(3. Not like) Na - maan or like John; graced by
(4. Wa-ter) flow - ing, flow - ing free, streams of

wa - ter flows for me. Cleans - ing wa - ter,
life and giv - ing birth; quench - ing thirst - y
God's own bless - ed Son. Wa - ter from his
wa - ter flows for me. Washed for - ev - er

WORDS: Gennifer Benjamin Brooks
MUSIC: Mark A. Miller

WATER BROOKS
77.77 55

Certainly, Lord

So those who welcomed his message were baptized,
and that day about three thousand persons were added. (Acts 2:41)

WORDS: African American spiritual
MUSIC: African American spiritual, arr. by Cynthia Wilson

Arr. © 2007 Abingdon Press, admin. by The Copyright Co.

CERTAINLY LORD
7 4 7 4 7 4 10

491

We Welcome You

*"Whoever welcomes you welcomes me,
and whoever welcomes me welcomes the one who sent me."* (Matthew 10:40)

See piano part to sing in three parts.

WORDS: Marilyn E. Thornton
MUSIC: Marilyn E. Thornton
© 2005 Marilyn E. Thornton

bread that comes from heaven. We wel - come you to the ta - ble of God. __
Ho - ly Spir - it's one. We love you with the love of God. __

Jesus Is Here Right Now

196

"For where two or three are gathered in my name, I am there among them." (Matthew 18:20)

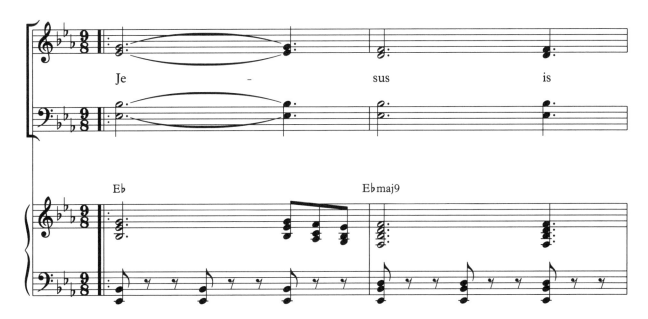

Je - sus is

WORDS: Leon Roberts
MUSIC: Leon Roberts

197

Glory to His Name

It is sown in dishonor, it is raised in glory. (1 Corinthians 15:43a)

WORDS: Elisha Hoffman
MUSIC: John H. Stockton, arr. by Monya Davis Logan

Arr. © 2007 Abingdon Press, admin. by The Copyright Co.

GLORY TO HIS NAME
999 7 with Refrain

Halleluya! Pelo Tsa Rona

For this I will extol you, O LORD, among the nations,
and sing praises to your name. (2 Samuel 22:50)

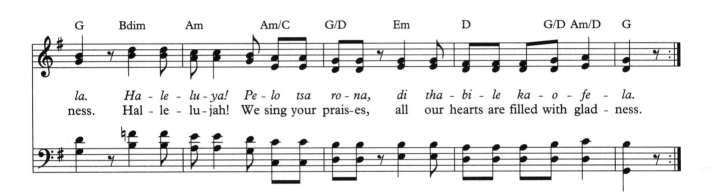

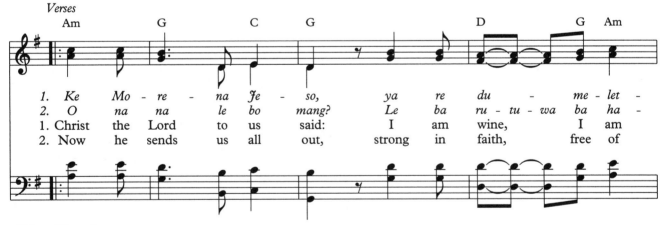

African Phonetics

Refrain
Hah-lay-loo-yah! Pay-loh tsah roh-nah, de tah-bil-lay kah-oh-fay-lay. *(twice)*

Verses
1. Kay Mow-ray-nah Jay-zoh, yah ray doo-may-layt-sang,
   yah ray doo-may-layt-sang, hoh tsah-may-sah ay-vahn-geh-dee.
2. Oh nah nah lay boh mahng? Lay bah-roo-too-wah bah hah-ay. *(twice)*

WORDS: South African spiritual (Sotho)
MUSIC: South African spiritual (Sotho)

498

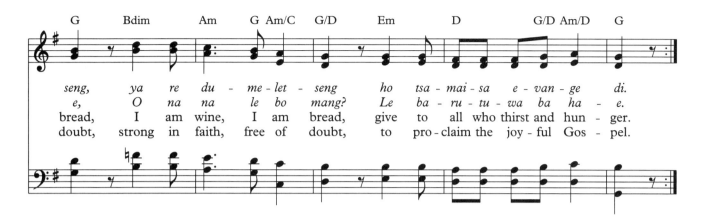

seng, ya re du - me - let - seng ho tsa - mai - sa e - van - ge di.
e, O na na le bo mang? Le ba - ru - tu - wa ba ha - e.
bread, I am wine, I am bread, give to all who thirst and hun - ger.
doubt, strong in faith, free of doubt, to pro - claim the joy - ful Gos - pel.

Broken for Me

199

And when he had given thanks, he broke it and said,
"This is my body that is for you." (1 Corinthians 11:24a)

Last time to Coda

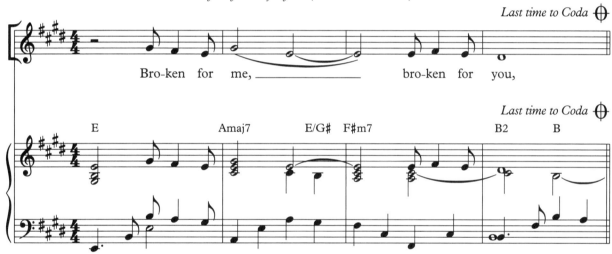

Bro-ken for me, _____ bro-ken for you,

Last time to Coda

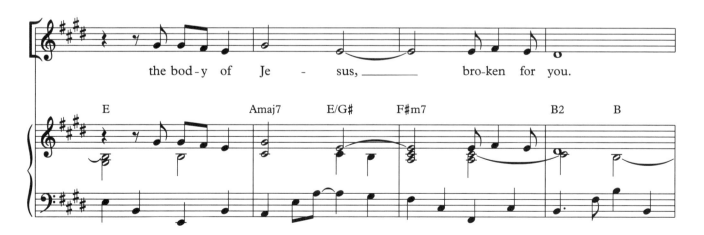

the bod-y of Je - sus, _____ bro-ken for you.

WORDS: Janet Lunt
MUSIC: Janet Lunt
© 1978 Sovereign Music UK

BROKEN FOR ME
Irregular with Refrain

A Perfect Sacrifice

He has appeared once for all at the end of the age
to remove sin by the sacrifice of himself. (Hebrews 9:26b)

1. Ho - ly One, _ Je - sus Christ, _ the on - ly One _
2. Lord I yield, _ yes I give _ this my song, _

_ wor - thy to give his life, _ for the sins of all man -
_ my praise of sac - ri - fice. I give you my life, you've al - read - y paid the

kind: such a per - fect sac - ri - fice, Je - sus Christ! _
price: such a per - fect sac - ri - fice, Je - sus Christ! _

WORDS: Michael McKay
MUSIC: Michael McKay, arr. by Nolan Williams, Jr.

201 I Know It Was the Blood

In him we have redemption through his blood, the forgiveness of our trespasses,
according to the riches of his grace. (Ephesians 1:7)

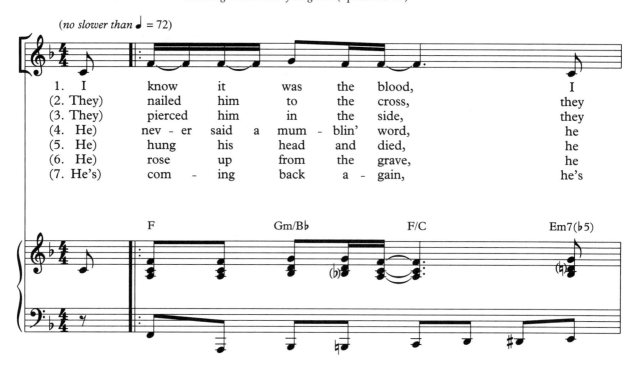

1. I know it was the blood,   I
(2. They) nailed him to the cross,   they
(3. They) pierced him in the side,   they
(4. He) nev - er said a mum - blin' word, he
(5. He) hung his head and died,   he
(6. He) rose up from the grave,   he
(7. He's) com - ing back a - gain,   he's

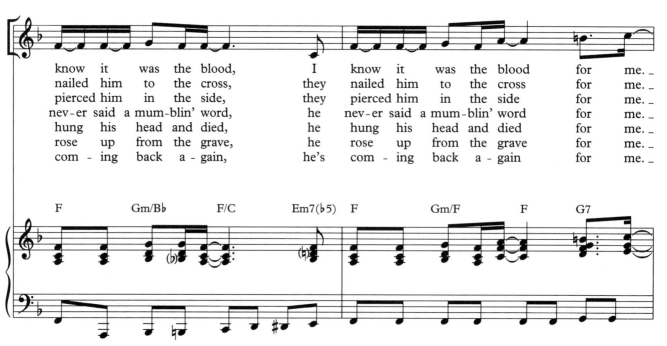

know it was the blood,   I know it was the blood for me. _
nailed him to the cross,   they nailed him to the cross for me. _
pierced him in the side,   they pierced him in the side for me. _
nev-er said a mum-blin' word, he nev-er said a mum-blin' word for me. _
hung his head and died,   he hung his head and died for me. _
rose up from the grave,   he rose up from the grave for me. _
com - ing back a - gain,   he's com - ing back a - gain for me. _

WORDS: Trad. African American
MUSIC: Trad. African American, arr. by Marilyn E. Thornton
Arr. © 2007 Abingdon Press, admin. by The Copyright Co.

IT WAS THE BLOOD
66 8 with Refrain

Grace Flows Down

From his fullness we have all received, grace upon grace. (John 1:16)

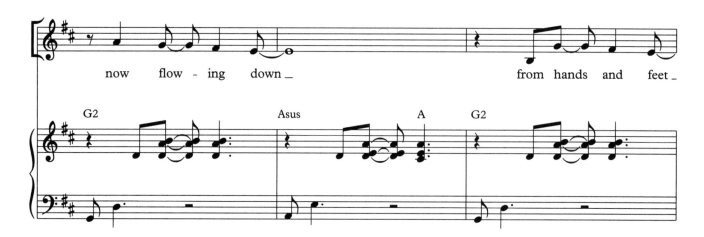

WORDS: David Bell, Louis Giglio, and Rod Padgett
MUSIC: David Bell, Louie Giglio, and Rod Padgett

it cov - ers me, _____

Asus   G2   G2

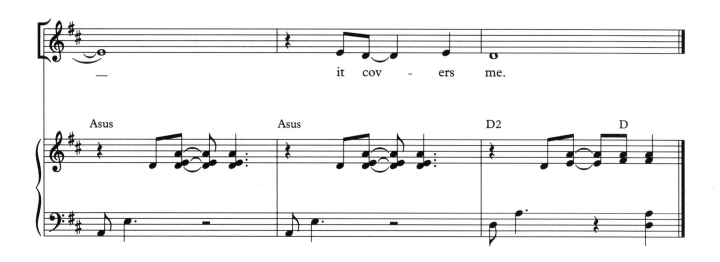

___ it cov - ers me.

Asus   Asus   D2   D

203

In Remembrance

"This cup is the new covenant in my blood.
Do this, as often as you drink it, in remembrance of me." (1 Corinthians 11:25b)

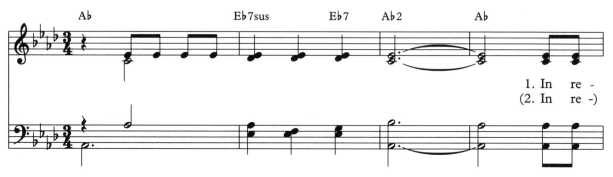

Ab   Eb7sus   Eb7   Ab2   Ab

1. In re -
(2. In re -)

WORDS: Ragan Courtney
MUSIC: Buryl Red

RED
Irregular

The Blood Will Never Lose Its Power

To him who loves us and freed us from our sins by his blood. (Revelation 1:5b)

WORDS: Andraé Crouch
MUSIC: Andraé Crouch

THE BLOOD
86 10 7 with Refrain

Taste and See

O taste and see that the LORD is good;
happy are those who take refuge in him. (Psalm 34:8)

Taste and see, taste and see the good - ness

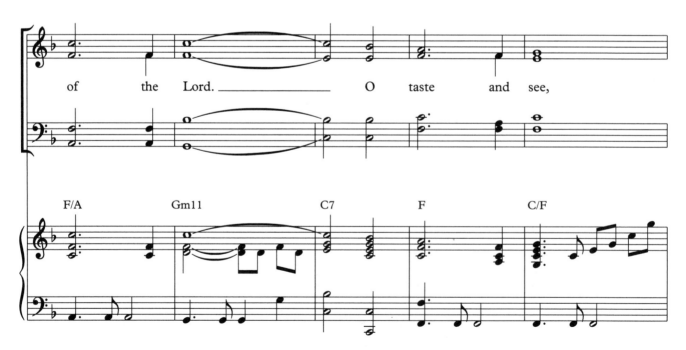

of the Lord. _____ O taste and see,

taste and see the good - ness of the Lord, _____ of the

Lord.

Lord.

To verses

Last time

To verses

Last time

Verses

1. I will bless the Lord at all times. _____
2. Glo - ri - fy the Lord with me. _____ To -
3. Wor - ship the Lord, all you peo - ple. _____

Bb/F   F   F/A   Bb2   F/A   Gm7   C7   C6   C7

F   Bb/F   F   Gm7/C   C7   F

F2   Am7   Bbmaj7   F/A

Let Us Talents and Tongues Employ

And all of them ate and were filled;
and they took up the broken pieces left over, seven baskets full. (Matthew 15:37)

1. Let us tal - ents and tongues em - ploy. Reach - ing out with a shout of joy:
2. Christ is a - ble to make us one. At the ta - ble he sets the tone,
3. Je - sus calls us in, sends us out bear - ing fruit in a world of doubt,

bread is bro - ken, the wine is poured, Christ is spo - ken and seen and heard.
teach - ing peo - ple to live to bless, love in word and in deed ex - press.
gives us love to tell, bread to share: God (Im-man - u - el) ev - ery - where!

Je - sus lives a - gain, earth can breathe a - gain, pass the word a - round: loaves a - bound!

WORDS: Fred Kaan
MUSIC: Jamaican folk melody, adapt. by Doreen Potter
© 1975 Hope Publishing Co.

LINSTEAD
LM with Refrain

207-a

Communion Setting

"Hosanna to the Son of David! Blessed is the one
who comes in the name of the Lord! Hosanna in the highest heaven!" (Matthew 21:9b)

(Preface)

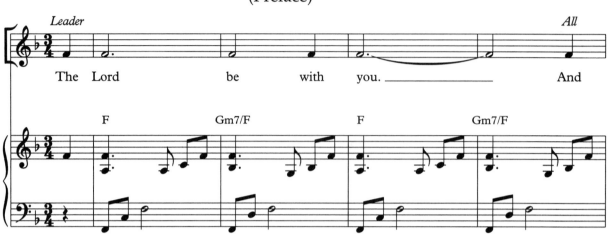

The Lord be with you. _____ And

al - so with you. _____ Lift

up your hearts. _____ We lift them up to the

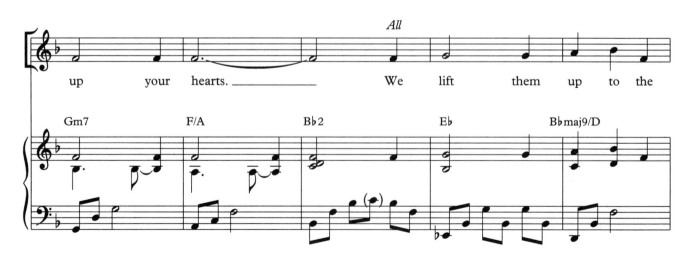

WORDS: From *The United Methodist Hymnal*
MUSIC: Mark A. Miller

Music © 2000 Abingdon Press, admin. by The Copyright Co.

(Sanctus)

207-b

WORDS: From *The United Methodist Hymnal* (Isa. 6:3; Matt. 21:9)
MUSIC: Mark A. Miller

(Memorial Acclamation) 207-c

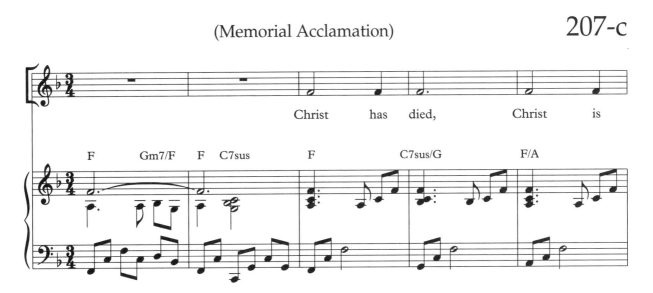

WORDS: From *The United Methodist Hymnal*
MUSIC: Mark A. Miller

ris - en, Christ will come a - gain. _____ Ho - san - na in the

high-est! Ho - san - na in the high-est! Ho - san - na in the high - est! _____

207-d
(Great Amen)

A - men. A -

WORDS: From *The United Methodist Hymnal*
MUSIC: Mark A. Miller

Music © 2000 Abingdon Press, admin. by The Copyright Co.; new arr. © 2007 Mark A. Miller

men.   A - men. _____ Ho - san - na in the

high-est! Ho - san - na in the high-est! Ho - san - na in the high - est! _____

O, How He Loves you and Me

"For God so loved the world that he gave his only Son,
so that everyone who believes in him may not perish but may have eternal life." (John 3:16)

1. O, how he loves you and me, _____
2. Je - sus to Cal - v'ry did go, _____

WORDS: Kurt Kaiser
MUSIC: Kurt Kaiser, arr. by William S. Moon
© 1975 Word Music, LLC

PATRICIA
Irregular

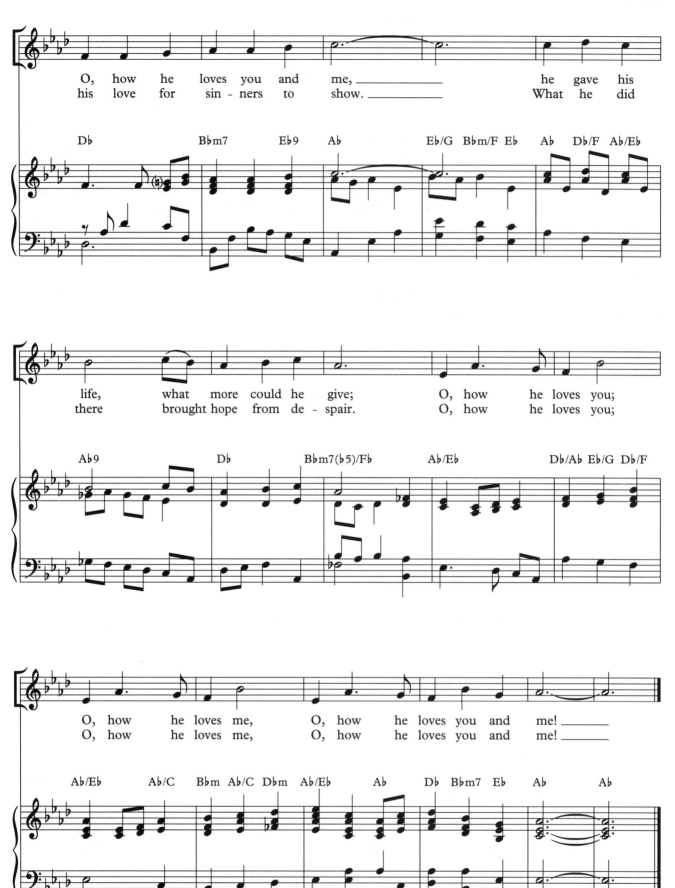

Psalm 19:14

Let the words of my mouth and the meditation of my heart be acceptable to you,
O LORD, my rock and my redeemer. (Psalm 19:14)

WORDS: Regina Hoosier
MUSIC: Regina Hoosier
© 2002 Regina Hoosier

210

Acceptable to You

Let the words of my mouth and the meditation of my heart be acceptable to you,
O LORD, my rock and my redeemer. (Psalm 19:14)

Not too slowly

WORDS: Eli Wilson, Jr.
MUSIC: Eli Wilson, Jr., arr. by Darryl Glenn Nettles

525

What Shall I Render?

What shall I return to the LORD for all his bounty to me? (Psalm 116:12)

WORDS: Margaret Pleasant Douroux
MUSIC: Margaret Pleasant Douroux

Offering

Present your bodies as a living sacrifice,
holy and acceptable to God, which is your spiritual worship. (Romans 12:1b)

Opt. guitar line - play throughout

See Performance Notes.

WORDS: Toby Hill
MUSIC: Toby Hill
© 2005 Toby Hill

213

We Bring the Sacrifice of Praise

*Through Jesus, therefore, let us continually offer to God a sacrifice of praise—
the fruit of lips that confess his name. (Hebrews 13:15 NIV)*

We bring the sac-ri-fice of praise in-to the house of the Lord.

We bring the sac-ri-fice of praise in-to the house of the Lord. And we

WORDS: Kirk Dearman
MUSIC: Kirk Dearman, arr. by Stephen Key

214 Praise God, from Whom All Blessings Flow

Praise the LORD! How good it is to sing praises to our God;
for he is gracious, and a song of praise is fitting. (Psalm 147:1)

Praise God, from whom all bless - ings flow;

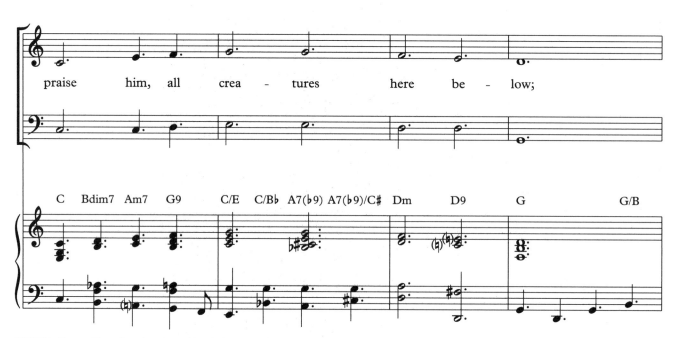

praise him, all crea - tures here be - low;

WORDS: Thomas Ken, adapt. from Isaac Watts and William Kethe
MUSIC: Adapt. from John Hatton by George Coles, arr. by Monya Davis Logan
© 1968 Roberta Martin

praise him a - bove, ye heav - en - ly host;

C Bdim7 Am7 G9 C/E C F E7 Am Am/C♯ G/D D7 C(4)/G C/D G7 G/B

praise Fa - ther, Son, and Ho - ly Ghost.

C C/G Gm11 C7 F A7(♯5) Dm11(♭5) Fm6 C/G C(♭5)/G G7sus G7 C

A - men. A - men.

F C/G F/A F2/B C F C/E Dm7 Bm7(♭5) C

215

God Be with You

May the grace of our Lord Jesus Christ be with your spirit,
brothers and sisters. Amen. (Galatians 6:18)

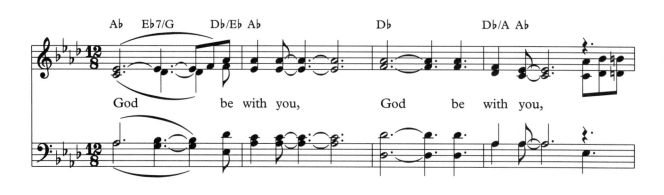

God be with you, God be with you,

God be with you, un-til we meet a - gain;

God be with you, God be with you,

God be with you, un-til we meet a - gain.

WORDS: Thomas A. Dorsey
MUSIC: Thomas A. Dorsey, arr. by Horace Clarence Boyer

If You Say Go

Now by this we may be sure that we know him, if we obey his commandments. (1 John 2:3)

WORDS: Diane Thiel
MUSIC: Diane Thiel, arr. by William S. Moon

Prepare Us, Lord

So we are ambassadors for Christ,
since God is making his appeal through us. (2 Corinthians 5:20a)

Pre - pare us, Lord, _____ to be your in - stru - ment; _____

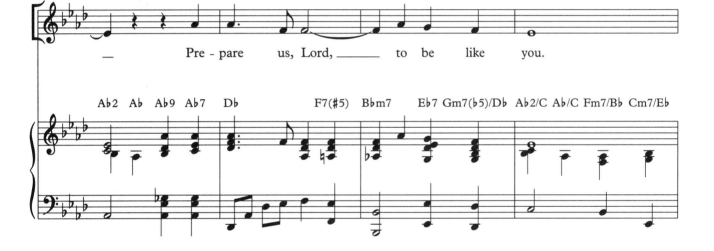

Pre - pare us, Lord, _____ to be like you.

Pre - pare us, Lord, _____ that we might tru - ly re - pre -

WORDS: Eli Wilson, Jr.
MUSIC: Eli Wilson, Jr.

© Eli Wilson, Jr.

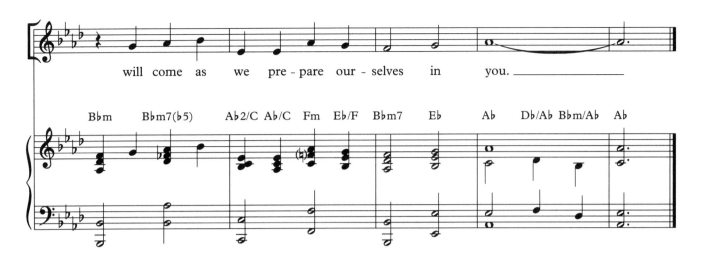

218

As You Go, Tell the World

As you go, proclaim the good news, "The kingdom of heaven has come near." (Matthew 10:7)

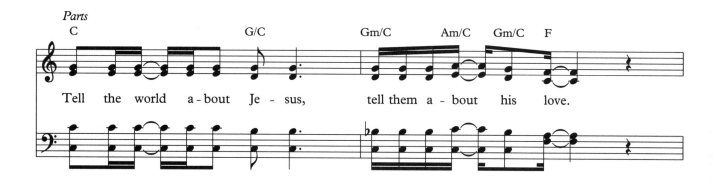

WORDS: Anonymous
MUSIC: Anonymous, arr. by Valeria A. Foster

I Need You to Survive

Above all, clothe yourselves with love . . . . And let the peace of Christ rule in your hearts,
to which indeed you were called in the one body. (Colossians 3:14-15a)

WORDS: David Frazier
MUSIC: David Frazier, arr. by Mark A. Miller

© God's Music

I love you, I need you to sur-vive. _

220   Honor and Glory

To the King of the ages, immortal, invisible, the only God,
be honor and glory forever and ever. Amen. (1 Timothy 1:17)

To the King e-ter - nal, im-mor - tal, in - vis-i-ble, the on - ly God, be the

hon-or and glo - ry for-ev - er and ev - er; to the

King e-ter - nal, im-mor - tal, in - vis - i-ble, the on - ly God, be the

WORDS: Gary Oliver
MUSIC: Gary Oliver

221 Alpha and Omega

"I am the Alpha and the Omega, the first and the last, the beginning and the end." (Revelation 22:13)

Reverently

You are Al - pha and O - me - ga, we wor - ship you, our Lord, you are wor - thy to be praised. _____ You are praised. _____ We give you all the glo - ry, we wor - ship you, our

Bbm Ab Gb Db/F Gb Ebm/Gb

Piano may play vocal parts softly.

WORDS: Erasmus Mutanbira
MUSIC: Trad. African, transcribed by William S. Moon

© 2005 Sound of the New Breed, admin. by Integrity's Praise! Music (BMI)

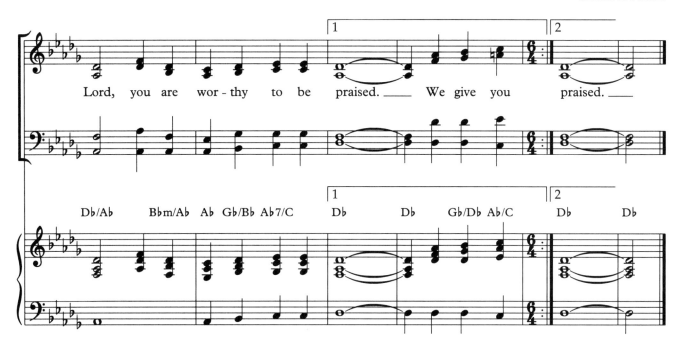

Lord, you are wor-thy to be praised. ____ We give you praised. ____

Db/Ab   Bbm/Ab Ab Gb/Bb Ab7/C   Db   Db   Gb/Db Ab/C   Db   Db

Acknowledgments

Use of copyrighted material is gratefully acknowledged by the publisher. Every effort has been made to locate the administrator of each copyright. The publisher would be pleased to have any errors or omissions brought to its attention. All copyright notices include the following declarations. All rights reserved. International copyright secured. Used with permission.

Abingdon Press (see The Copyright Company)

Doris Akers (see Unichappell Music)

Albert E. Brumley & Sons (see ICG)

Alfred Publishing, P.O. Box 10003, Van Nuys, CA 91410-0003

Amity Music

Ariose Music (see EMI CMG Publishing)

Augsburg Fortress Publishers, P.O. Box 1209, Minneapolis, MN 55440-1209; (612) 330-3300

B4 Entertainment, Rich Burchell, P.O. Box 331423, Murfreesboro, TN 37133; (615) 217-4711; rickyb@b4entertainment.com

BMG (ASCAP) (see Music Services)

BMG Songs, Inc. (see Music Services)

Birdwing Music (see EMI CMG Publishing)

Bob Jay Publishing, c/o Rodney L. Adams, P.O. Box 515, Lincolnton Station, New York, NY 10037-0514; (212) 283-4980; Bobjay7412@aol.com

Boosey & Co. (see Boosey & Hawkes, Inc.)

Boosey & Hawkes, Inc., 35 East 21st St., New York, NY 10010; (212) 358-5300

Brentwood-Benson Music Publishing, Inc. (see Music Services)

Bridge Building Music (see Brentwood-Benson Music Publishing)

Broadman Press (see Van Ness Press)

Gennifer Benjamin Brooks, Garrett Evangelical Theology Seminary, 2121 Sheridan Rd., Evanston, IL 60201

Bud John Songs (see EMI CMG Publishing)

Bud John Tunes, Inc. (see EMI CMG Publishing)

CMI-HP Publishing (see Word Music, LLC)

Caribbean Conference of Churches, P.O. Box 867, Port of Spain, Trinidad; (866) 623-0588; trinidad-headoffice@ccc-caribe.org

Carlin America, 126 East 38th St., New York, NY 10016

Carol Joy Music (see ICG)

Century Oak Publishing Group (see MCS America)

Changing Church Forum, 13901 Fairview Dr., Burnsville, MN 55337; (800) 874-2044, FAX (612) 435-8015; changing@changingchurch.org

Michael L. Charles, 5717 NE Quartz Dr., Lees Summit, MO 64064

Chinwah Songs (see Executive Publishing Administration)

Cecilia L. Clemons; c/o Tracyton United Methodist Church; P.O. Box 127; Tracyton, WA 98393

J. Jefferson Cleveland, Estate of J. Jefferson Cleveland, c/o William B. McCain, 4500 Massachusetts Ave. NW, Washington, DC 20016

Colette Coward, 336 Meadow Glen Drive, Bear, DE 19701

Crouch Music (see EMI CMG Publishing)

Pamela Jean Davis, 1502 Fountain Lake Dr., #627, Stafford, TX 77477

Dayspring Music, LLC (see Word Music, LLC)

Dixon Music, Rev. Jessy Dixon, 3240 Danne Rd., Crete, IL 60417; (708) 672-8682

Donn Charles Thomas Publishing, Messiah's World Outreach Ministries, P.O. Box 594, Stone Mountain, GA 30086; (404) 299-8005; dthomas801@aol.com

Doulos Publishing (see Maranatha! Music)

Dr. Margaret Pleasant Douroux, Rev. Earl Pleasant Publishing, P.O. Box 3247, Thousand Oaks, CA 91359; (818) 991-3728, FAX (818) 991-2567

Jonathan Cole Dow, c/o Aldersgate Renewal Ministries, 121 East Ave., Goodlettsville, TN 37072

EMI CMG Publishing, P.O. Box 5085, Brentwood, TN 37024-5085

Edward B. Marks Music Co. (see Carlin America)

Executive Publishing Administration, 10220 Glade Ave., Chatsworth, CA 91311

Full Armor Music (see The Kruger Organization)

Gaither Copyright Management, P.O. Box 737, Alexandria, IN 46001; (765) 724-8233, FAX (765) 724-8290

Gamut Music Productions, 704 Saddle Trail Ct., Hermitage, TN 37076

General Board of Global Ministries (see Hope Publishing)

GIA Publications, Inc., 7404 S. Mason Ave., Chicago, IL 60638; (708) 496-3800

God's Music, c/o Li'l Dave's Music, 6 Gramaton Ave., 5th Floor, Mount Vernon, NY 10550

Grace Fellowship (see Maranatha! Music)

Hal Leonard, P.O. Box 13819, Milwaukee, WI 53213

Harvest Fire Music (see Integrity's Praise! Music)

Toby Hill, 7410 Oak Walk Dr., Humble, TX 77346

Hillsongs Publishing (see Integrity Music)

Hope Publishing Company, 380 S. Main Pl., Carol Stream, IL 60188; (800) 323-1049, FAX (630) 665-2552; www.hopepublishing.com

Regina Hoosier, P.O. Box 30094, Clarksville, TN 37040; yielded@bellsouth.net

House Of Mercy Music (see Music Services)

J. Edward Hoy

ICG, P.O. Box 24149, Nashville, TN 37202

Integrity Music, Inc., 1000 Cody Rd., Mobile, AL 36695-3425; (334) 633-9000, FAX (334) 633-9998

Intergrity's Hosanna! Music (see Integrity Music, Inc.)

Intergrity's Praise! Music (see Integrity Music, Inc.)

International Atlanta Music (see Malaco Music)

JDI Music (see JRobersongs Music)

Jeff Ferguson Music (see ICG)

John T. Benson Publishing Co. (see Music Services)

Jonathan Mark Music (see Gaither Copyright Management)

JRobersongs Music, P.O. Box 48105, Los Angeles, CA 90048

K Cartunes Music (see Lilly Mack Music)

Kevin Mayhew Ltd., Buxhall, Stowmarket, Suffolk, UK IP14 3DJ

Kingsman's Thankyou Music (see EMI CMG Publishing)

Latter Rain Music (see EMI CMG Publishing)

Lehsem Songs (see ICG)

Leon Lewis, 10500 Fountain Lake Dr., Stafford, TX 77477

Life Song Music Press (see Music Services)

Life Spring Music, 907 McCall St., Conroe, TX 77301

Lifeway Christian Resources, One Lifeway Plaza MSN160, Nashville, TN 37234

Lilly Mack Music (BMI), 421 E. Beach, Inglewood, CA 90302; (310) 677-5603, FAX (310) 677-0250

Monya Davis Logan, 3810 York St., Dallas, TX 75210-2736

Ludlow Music, Inc., c/o The Richmond Organization, 266 West 37th Street, 17th Floor, New York, NY 10018-6609

MCS America, 1625 Broadway, 4th Floor, Nashville, TN 37203; janice.bain@mcsamerica.net

MWP Publishing (see JRobersongs Music)

Malaco Music, P.O. Box 9287, Jackson, MS 39286-9281; (601) 982-4522, FAX (601) 982-4528

Manna Music, 35255 Brooten Rd., Pacific City, OR 97135; (503) 965-6112

Maranatha! Music (see Music Services)

Maranatha! Praise, Inc. (see Music Services)

Martha Munizzi Music (see Say The Name Publishing)

Roberta Martin (see Unichappell Music)

Martin and Morris Studio, Inc. (see Unichappell Music)

Patrick Matsikenyiri, No. 13 Cripps Rd., Palmerton, Mutare, Zimbabwe; (540) 514-6359

Meadowgreen Music (see EMI CMG Publishing)

Meaux Mercy (see EMI CMG Publishing)

Mercy/Vineyard Music (see Music Services)

Mark A. Miller, 1118 Gresham Rd., Plainfield, NJ 07062

Mo' Berrie Publishing, P.O. Box 818, Summit, MS 39666 (601) 684-0117

William S. Moon, 909 Halcyon Avenue, Nashville, TN 37204

Mountain Spring Music (see EMI CMG Publishing)

Music Services, Inc. (ASCAP), 1526 Otter Creek Rd., Nashville, TN 37215

New Song Music, P.O. Box 116, Lawai, HI 96765

New Spring Publishing (see Brentwood-Benson Music Publishing)

Verolga Nix, 931 E. Sedgwick St., Philadelphia, PA 19150-3517; (215) 248-2728

Nory B Publishing (see Malaco Music)

Johnetta Johnson Page, 4927 Silen Lake Dr., San Antonio, TX 78244

Paragon Music (seee Brentwood-Benson Music Publishing)

Raise Publishing Co., Raymond Wise, 197 Monarch Dr., Pataskala, OH 43062

Richwood Music (see MCS America)

Ron Harris Music, c/o Ron Harris, 22643 Paul Revere Dr., Calabasas, CA 91302

Sanabella Music (see EMI CMG Publishing)

Say The Name Publishing, c/o Nick Kroger, 575 Dunmar Circle, Winter Springs, FL 32708-3905; (407) 834-5620, FAX (407) 673-5620; saythename@hotmail.com

Schaff Music Publishing, 14 Sullivans Lane, Missouri City, TX 77459

Scripture in Song (see Maranatha! Music)

Shepherd's Heart Music (see Dayspring Music, LLC)

sixsteps music (see EMI CMG Publishing)

Sound III (see Universal Music)

Sound of Gospel

Sound of the New Breed (see Integrity's Praise! Music)

Sovereign Grace Praise (see Integrity's Praise! Music)

Sovereign Music UK, P.O. Box 356, Leighton Buzzard, BEDS, LU7 8WP, UK; sovereignm@aol.com

Spoone Music (see Word Music, LLC)

Stamps-Baxter Music (see Brentwood-Benson Music Publishing)

Straightway Music (see EMI CMG Publishing)

T. Autumn Music (see Zomba Songs)

TMMI (see Music Services)

Tedd T BMI Publishing Designed (see EMI CMG Publishing)

The Church of God in Christ Publishing Board

The Copyright Company, 1025 16th Ave. South, Suite 204, Nashville, TN 37212; FAX (615) 244-5591; lynda.pearson@thecopyrightco.com

The Iona Community (Scotland) (see GIA Publications, Inc.)

The Kruger Organization, Inc., 15 Rolling Way, New York, NY 10956-6912; (202) 966-3280, FAX (202) 364-1367; publishing@tkgoup.com

The United Methodist Publishing House (see The Copyright Company)

Marilyn E. Thornton, The United Methodist Publishing House, 201 8th Ave. South, Nashville, TN 37202

Cecilia Olusola Tribble, c/o Marilyn E. Thornton, The United Methodist Publishing House, 201 8th Ave. South, Nashville, TN 37202

Unichappell Music (see Alfred Publishing)

Universal MCA Music Publishing (see Universal Music)

Universal Music Publishing (see Hal Leonard)

Utryck (see Walton Music Group)

Van Ness Press (see Lifeway Christian Resources)

Vineyard Songs (see Music Services)

WGRG The Iona Community (Scotland) (see GIA Publications, Inc.)

Walton Music Group, 1028 Highland Woods Rd., Chapel Hill, NC 27517; (919) 929-1330

Wayne Leupold Editions, 8510 Triad Dr., Colfax, NC 27235

Warner-Tamerlane Publishing (see Alfred Publishing)

We Lyke Music, 3001 West 82nd Pl., Inglewood, CA 90305

Wendell Whalum, The Estate of Wendell Whalum, c/o Clarie Whalum, 2439 Greenwood Circle, East Point, GA 30344

Whole Armor Music (see The Kruger Organization)

Willow Branch Publishing (see Gaither Copyright Management)

Brian C. Wilson, 1811 Villa Del Lago, Missouri City, TX 77459

Cynthia Wilson, 2786 Keystone Ave., Lithonia, GA 30058

Eli Wilson, Jr., Eli Wilson Ministries, P.O. Box 680172, Orlando, FL 32868-0712

Word Music, LLC, 20 Music Square East, Nashville, TN 37203; (615) 733-1880, FAX (615) 733-1885; luann.inman@warnerchappell.com

worshiptogether.com songs (see EMI CMG Publishing)

Wythrne Music (see JRobersongs Music)

Y'Shua Publishing

Darlene Zschech (see Integrity Music)

Performance Notes

General Notes

Some songs are sung at a slower tempo in African American churches, less peppy and with more reverence. These include songs 15, 40, 53, and 165.

A "bump" can be described as using a percussion instrument (including hand clapping) to place the heavier pulse on the weaker beat in a song that has a medium to slow tempo. A song in 12/8 time is usually interpreted as being in FOUR, with each dotted half note receiving one beat. To create a "bump," the second and fourth beats will receive the heavier emphasis.

The "lilt" or "lift" is a lighter version of the "bump," occurring in THREE meter. While the principle beat receives the heavier pulse, there is an emphasis on the weak beat. In the case of 3/4 time, add percussion to the second and third quarter notes. In the case of songs in 6/8, 9/8, and sometimes 12/8, add percussion on every second and third eighth note. Songs that need a bump or lilt (may already be indicated) are: 41, 62, 66, 77, 124, 128, 137, 161, 167, 172, 173, 190, 196, 197, 204, and 215.

Praise and Adoration—God's Omnipresence

1. All Around Me!

This song can be done very upbeat or at a medium tempo. It is very effective with these movements:

1. God is high (*lift arms up*)
   God is low (*point arms down*)
   God is wide (*stretch arms out*)
   and he loves me so (*hug self*)
   All around me (*twirl right*)
   Oh yes, all around me (*twirl left*)
   So high (*arms up*)
   so low (*arms down*)
   so wide (*arms out*)
   And he loves me so (*hug*)

2. God is here (*point in front of self*)
   God is there (*point to other side of room*)
   God is great (*arms up*)
   and he's ev'rywhere (*point in many directions*)
   All around me (*twirl right*)
   Oh yes, all around me (*twirl left*)
   So here (*point in front*)
   so there (*point away*)
   so great (*arms up*)
   And everywhere (*many directions*)

3. God is in (*point to heart*)
   God is out (*point away from self*)
   God's so good (*hug self*)
   and it makes me SHOUT (*pump arms*)
   All around me (*twirl right*)
   Oh yes, all around me (*twirl left*)
   So in (*heart*)
   so out (*point away*)
   so good (*hug*)
   and it makes me SHOUT (*pump arms*)

© 2006 Cecilia Olusola Tribble

2. All My Days

Note: If hands are free, encourage congregation to clap.

Praise and Adoration—God's Omnipotence

13. What a Mighty God We Serve

A percussive rhythm of eighth notes undergirds this selection.

Praise and Adoration—God's Providence

17. God Made Me

While the original rhythm for the verses are included, the leader may improvise on the rhythm. Allow the congregation to practice the clapping at the end of the refrain and the responses in bridges 1 and 2 before this selection is presented.

22. I Will Sing unto the Lord

To be sung as a canon, divide the congregation into three groups. Then have the entire congregation sing the selection all the way through. Start over with group 1 singing measures 1–4: "I will sing unto the Lord." They will continue to sing these measures only as group 2 enters singing the section that begins with "The Lord, my God my strength, my song." Groups 1 and 2 will sing their assigned part as group 3 enters with "The Lord is God and I will praise God." Repeat as desired.

Praise and Adoration—The Name of Jesus Christ

25. Glorious Is the Name

The second section may be performed with rhythmic liberty at the desire of the worship leader or choir director. It may be done slower, with holds and pauses in appropriate places, as desired.

29–33. Name Medley

"Praise the Name" (29), "Bless That Wonderful Name of Jesus" (30), and "In the Name of Jesus" (32) are in the same tempo. You may choose to group them together. You may also choose to pair "His Name Is Wonderful" (31) with "Jesus, What a Beautiful Name" (33) or place both of these slower selections at the end of the medley.

Praise and Adoration—Honoring Jesus Christ

34. In the Sanctuary

The congregation will enjoy participating. Encourage the people to lift and clap their hands as the lyrics suggest. Repeat measures 21–28 ("Yes, yes, Lord for the rest of our days") as desired. Allow worship participants to self-select their vocal parts, and voice by voice, starting with the sopranos, learn each part separately with all voices combining when the worship leader gives the direction to do so.

Praise and Adoration—The Sacrifice of Jesus Christ

38. Celebrator

Allow the instruments to set the tempo by repeating the first two measures without vocals as desired for an introduction. Each section can be repeated as desired by the worship leader. To vary the repetitions:

1. Have the women imitate the bass line motive (sixteenth rest, 3 sixteenth notes, quarter note), singing da-da-da-da on B-flat, starting with the fourth beat of measure 8.

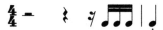

2. Starting in measure 14 (second section) the men can answer back "Oh!" on the fourth beat of every measure.

Praise and Adoration—Sanctifying Grace

42. Lord, Reign in Me

Percussion may create polyrhythms that are inclusive of a heavy accent on the & of the second and fourth beats.

Praise and Adoration—The Joy of the Lord

50. Show Teeth

This selection is a conversation between one or two soloists, the congregation, and a vocal trio. Encourage all to show their teeth and smile with joy!

52. Incredible

To extend, divide the congregation into two groups. Have one group repeatedly sing the "ohs" from measures 1–4. Have the second group join the first while singing repeatedly, "We reach and you grab hold," at measures 41–44. Repeat as desired. Then have the two groups exchange parts. End the song with all singing "We reach!"

Jesus Christ—His Birth

53. All Hail King Jesus

Some congregations prefer to sing this up-tempo and victoriously, however, many African American congregations prefer this slower, more stately tempo.

Jesus Christ—His Resurrection

77. Raised, He's Been Raised from the Dead

After the first verse is sung, it will be very effective to have a soloist improvising, starting with the refrain.

Living the Faith—Ministry

94. Step (For Ushers)

In many African American churches, the ushers have a marching ritual. After lifting the offering pew by pew, they gather in the back to march down the aisles to the sound of upbeat music in the process of bringing the plates/baskets to the front. If the practice of lifting the offering includes the entire congregation bringing their offering to the plates/baskets in the front of the church, the ushers may march down to bring their personal offering after everyone else is finished. Often, they will march with a specially designed step. They may have on white gloves and do hand movements as well. This song was created to honor this step tradition, which was passed down from Africa and has variations in marching bands and fraternal groups on college campuses. Youth and children's choirs will enjoy singing this song as a processional and creating their own steps.

Living the Faith—Healing

118. Come On in My Room

While this selection is not a historical African American spiritual, it should be sung with the feeling of the blues. In fact, the harmonies the arranger, Cecilia Clemons, used indicate the flatted third that is played simultaneously with major chords (see measures 5, 7, and 10). This is a throwback to the bent note phenomenon of blues singing. Additionally the word "my" is spelled in most cases "ma." On short notes, it could just as easily be "muh" or m'.

Living the Faith—Revival

120. Father, I Stretch My Hands to Thee

In metering or "lining out" this hymn, the first phrase is spoken or chanted by one person before everyone responds (from *Songs of Zion*, p. xvi).

121. Higher, Higher

This selection can be done with hand and body movements.

> Stanza 1: Pumping uplifted hands towards heaven
> Stanza 2: Pushing hands downward and bending the knees
> Stanza 3: Making fists and pushing arms forward.

Living the Faith—Thanksgiving

126. I Remember

This selection is a twenty-first-century "call and response" format. It calls for two rappers and two groups of people. The two groups can be choir and congregation or some other division. Assign the congregation voice 2 of the refrain, "I remember," which is actually the "response" even though it occurs first. Eventually, the congregation will begin to repeat the other words for the refrain, but allow a group, such as the choir to do voice 1 of the refrain, which is actually the "call." The voice 2 rapper can invite the people to join in at any time with "I remember."

Order of Service—Call to Worship

142. Come, Come! Ev'rybody Come!

Three-part vocal harmony can be improvised using the right hand of the piano accompaniment as a guide.

Order of Service—Prayer

155. Heavenly Father

This selection seems to be very long and difficult but can be simplified.

1. Rap 1 can be done by an individual, the congregation or a small group. It recurs several times and contains the essence of the message of the prayer.
2. Rap 2 should be learned and performed by an individual. It paraphrases parts of the Lord's Prayer and tells a story of confession and repentance.
3. Teach the unison sections to the congregation as a prayer chant. As the selection goes along, members of the congregation can choose whether they will sing the unison part or say rap 1.
4. The other sung parts can be learned by small groups of singers. There are unison parts that move between male and female voices and a section for a trio of voices. Include the trio only as part of a choral production.

Refrain

I come in the name of your Son,
asking to be forgiven for the things that I've done.
In my life I need you now more than ever,
and in my life I need you to make things better.

Heavenly Father, Abba, hallowed be thy name
Thy Kingdom come, and your will be done.
It's your child, I come, I'm messed up, Lord,
I've been fighting this battle and I've been cut and sore.
And I need to turn to you because your love is true,
I want to turn the page of my life to Chapter Two.
But I'm slippin' and fallin', and I want to get up,
but the devil's holding me down and I want to give up.

But I want back in your grace, I want back in your
  mercy,
I want to live a life for God, but I ain't worthy.
But they say the ones that call upon your name,
That you won't forsake them and they will be saved.
So I pray to you, I want to come back home,
because these burdens on my shoulders are just
  weighing me down.
So forgive me as I forgive them that trespass against
  me.
Show me the way, show me your path.

Chorus (sung)
Heavenly Father, Lord, I need you
In my life, in my life.

Refrain (in the background)
I come in the name of your Son,
asking to be forgiven for the things that I've done.
In my life I need you now more than ever,
and in my life I need you to make things better.

Now I'm down in the dirt and deep inside the gutter
but I know that your path, your ways are always better.
You got true love that comes from up above
that gets me higher than any drink or any drug.
I coming to you but you seem so far away,
and I know I made it this far because of your grace.
So praise, be unto you, my God,
I worship, I love you, heavenly Father.

Chorus and Refrain

I know every time I call that you hear me,
so this time I'm just leaning on your mercy.
The earthy, the worldly, I give up. Change me,
'cause Heavenly Father, you the one that made me.
Save me, I pray thee, Jesus you gave me.
For dying for my sins, the wages, you paid it.
And your mercy is good everyday.
Thank you, Heavenly Father, in the name of Jesus I
      pray.

Chorus and Refrain

Order of Service—Response to the Word

181. He's My Foundation

This selection works well as a companion to no. 182 "The Solid Rock" or by using the refrain as an antiphon between the verses of the hymn "The Church's One Foundation" (*The United Methodist Hymnal,* no. 545). Keep the same tempo when using it as an antiphon.

185. Never Been Scared

Congregations inclusive of all ages have been very excited about this selection. The refrain or chorus appears on the last three pages of this selection (pp. 471–73). Teach this part to the congregation first. All the people say is: "I ain't never been scared." You may want to have two to four rappers.

Order of Service—Offering

212. Offering

Teach this to your congregation by having the praise team sing short phrases and allowing the people echo them.

Index of Scripture

Topical Index

Index of Composers, Arrangers, Authors, Translators, and Sources

Index of First Lines and Common Titles

ISBN-13: 978-0-687-33537-4

90000

9 780687 335374